Celebrations to Remember

Exceptional Party Decor and Fabulous Food

Parties and Pictures by Soile Anderson

Words by Eleanor Ostman

Cover and page design by Kimberlea Weeks, Sexton Creative

Printed by Sexton Printing, Inc., St. Paul, MN

ISBN 978-0-692-81985-2

Printed and bound in the United States of America

Cover photo of Soile Anderson by Alicia Griffin Mills

contents

Page 24

Page 63

Page 38

Page 70

Page 74

Page 13

"Planning a party proceeds best if you define the purpose and select a theme. Then the decor and menu fall into place."

Soile's Story

You are reading the improbable tale of how Soile Anderson, raised in eastern Finland near Savonlinna and brought up "big time" in the Lutheran tradition, has become the most sought-after Kosher caterer in Minnesota. The Jewish celebrations she stages are legendary, not only for her creative approach to cooking within the boundaries of Kosher rules, but also for the dazzling décor that make her parties distinctive. With her own photos, recipes and advice, Soile shares ideas selected from 30 years of her Deco Catering company, working in the Midwest and beyond, for unforgettable parties and weddings. Wait until you see what she can do! And that you can do, as well.

HOW SOILE'S COOKING CAREER BEGAN

Young Soile learned about food early in life. "My mother was a superb cook and baker. Our house always had the best aromas coming from the wood burning oven." As the oldest of four siblings, whose father died when she was seven as a result of earlier wartime injuries, Soile needed to help her widowed mother in the kitchen. "I would call it healthy home cooking, using fresh berries, mushrooms and produce from our large garden," she recalls. "I always wanted to help my mother, and sometimes she would get irritated with me because I was always at her elbow." She hovered while her mother made traditional savory Karelian pies, cardamom-flavored Finn

bread called Pulla, and lavish Helsinki tortes. Soile continues to use her mother's family recipes

After high school, Soile began studies in hotel and restaurant management in Finland. Meanwhile, she married at 19, and by the time she was 22, she was mother to two sons. In her spare moments she often watched American cowboy movies and was fascinated with wagon wheels, Indians and other western symbols. While pushing a baby carriage on her daily morning run, she noticed a local restaurant in her hometown was available. She decided to open a Wild West restaurant, unlike anything in Finland before.

She got wood scraps free from a nearby factory to build tables and decorate the interior. Using rope and wagon wheels, swinging doors and birch bark light fixtures — "all very natural and earthy," she recalls — Soile opened Saluna (the Finnish word for saloon). It became an instant success for dining a long way from Texas or Colorado, so popular that customers had to buy advance tickets to get in the door. The staff wore western jeans and shirts, and South American musicians played for dancing. "We served very Finnish food — moose soup, reindeer roast, rabbit stew and local fish."

Soile's restaurant success inspired Savonlinna's mayor and local businessmen to suggest she and her husband build a hotel-spa complete with indoor swimming pool. At just age 26, she saw the possibilities. Using logs cut from the lakeside property, the couple built what would become a mecca where veterans, funded by the Finnish government, could receive wintertime rehabilitation services. In summer, the young owners catered to international tourists attracted by the local opera festival.

Despite the hotel's success, Soile determined to leave Finland and explore new opportunities in the fast-casual food business in America, perhaps to bring those ideas back to Finland. After she arrived in Minnesota, her first Twin Cities kitchen job was at a Perkins to learn American culture. She soon added a night shift at the upscale Anchorage restaurant in Roseville where she worked under the tutelage of master chef Klaus Mitterhaus.

She barely spoke English. "In school, I studied German and Swedish," she said. A newfound friend, Marjatta Gabriel, helped Soile master the language and made her feel more at home in the country she decided to adopt. Though she is now fully-conversant in English, thanks to Marjatta's coaching, Soile's Finnish accent remains distinctive.

Marjatta also found Soile a job at a newly-opening restaurant in Edina's Galleria shopping center. The owners of The French Loaf, Sue and Zack Sell, quickly realized Soile's abilities and offered her the job of kitchen manager, which became an excellent learning experience dealing with food purveyors and staff. By this time, her boys had arrived in America and were happily enrolled in the Edina school system.

David Speer, who, though not a Finn himself, was the honorary Finnish Consul in Minneapolis in the 1980s. On a trip to Finland, he happened to visit the hotel-spa and was impressed. Learning that former owner Soile was in Minnesota, he contacted her and suggested a job opportunity. She got a green card, and with Speer's encouragement and banking connections, in 1982, she got a loan and became the chef-owner of a restaurant in the Women's City Club (later the Minnesota Museum of Art) in St. Paul. The Deco-style building prompted the name of her restaurant there, Deco. Her Sunday Scandinavian brunches and elegant lunches were soon drawing crowds, as were evening banquets and weddings she catered. That was the beginning of her Deco Catering business.

"In just a couple of years, so much happened. The restaurant took off," she recalls.

In 1991, the Minnesota Museum of Art building which had housed Deco was sold and she had one year to move. She did research to expand her business, and realized how much demand there was for the baked goods she made while at Deco. In the St. Paul suburb of North Oaks, she relocated Deco Catering and opened her first Taste of Scandinavia bakery in 1992, which eventually expanded to four locations. A decade later, three of those Taste sites were sold to the Festival Foods grocery chain, but she kept the Como Avenue space, where she changed the name to Finnish Bistro. Deco Catering continued to thrive and she kept that business, moving production kitchens to a Hennepin Avenue warehouse in Minneapolis.

"Coming to the U.S. opened my eyes. I feel I have two wonderful countries, but I really love the business world here," Soile says. "Constant creativity is my life. I wake up each morning wondering what I can do today. Most everything is fascinating — except studying English grammar!"

Some caterers might not bother fashioning tomato roses or squash flowers to garnish plates, "but I like to have my food look beautiful and exciting and I'm willing to make that extra step."

She loved what she did at Deco, but after 30 years, it was time to retire; she sold it in 2015. Her son, Heikki Rouvinen, who has been her Deco partner for 14 years, remains with the new owners as an investor and partner. It continues to flourish.

Catering for Grand Celebrities and Great Customers

"I have been so blessed!"

Indeed she has. After she was honored to do a vegetarian menu for the Dalai Lama visiting Minnesota, he blessed Soile and her catering crew, and gifted her with a white scarf that she treasures.

When President Barack Obama came to the Twin Cities for a private party at Sam and Sylvia Kaplan's home (Kaplan was U.S. Ambassador to Morocco), Soile was thrilled to be tapped as caterer to serve 70 VIP guests at a sit-down dinner.

Soile was pleased when the President lauded her for 30 years of small business accomplishments and providing employment for hundreds of people. He personally thanked each crew member and chatted about their backgrounds.

King Harald and Queen Sylvia of Norway have dined on Deco fare. So have guests of Vice-President Walter Mondale and his wife, Joan, at their private home parties.

Soile and her specialty, Scandinavian smörgåsbord, were featured on The Food Network, extolled by host Alton Brown, and she appeared on *Martha Stewart Living* magazine pages. She has done cooking demonstrations on Twin Cities TV.

Minnesota governors and their wives frequently asked Soile and her crew to cater events at the state's official residence, and guests at Eastcliff, the home of University of Minnesota presidents, often dined on Deco delights.

Numerous law firms such as Minneapolis-based Dorsey and Whitney, call when they're having in-house events. Marilyn Nelson, former president of Carlson Companies and the Radisson Hotel Group, has asked Soile to arrange parties, as far-distant as in Jackson Hole, Wyoming.

It's exciting to do parties for celebrities, but Soile is most grateful to have legions of devoted customers, some into the second generation, who have been supportive of her business over three decades.

"I am so lucky, so thankful. My customers are loyal and wonderful," she says.

The Scandinavian community of Minneapolis-St. Paul calls on her to prepare their feasts, especially Swedish, Danish, Norwegian and Finnish holiday events.

And since she was first coaxed by Sue Kaplan to become competent and licensed in Kosher catering, she has gained another collection of faithful clients. "It has been so wonderful to get to know the Jewish culture," she says of that connection.

Soile's gratitude is far-reaching. She lauds floral designers such as Cindie Sinclair, Martha's Garden and Greg at Richfield Flowers "who can create according to any theme I might imagine." She is also grateful to Twin Cities food maven and columnist Sue Zelickson "who has been so supportive and lined up many events for me." She recalls one of the earlier ones, a huge event at the newly-opened Saks Fifth Avenue store in downtown Minneapolis. "I was nervous about it — a bunch of Finnish ladies putting on an African party — but Sue said we could do it — and we did."

Loyalty built Deco Catering — from customers who were devoted to Soile and the events she planned, and from her hard-working staff of cooks and servers who made every party perfect. She is so grateful to everyone, especially her son Heikki Rouvinen, who continues with Deco Catering, handling complex business aspects of the company.

Though the ideas, photos and recipes for the book were Soile's, she worked from inception to completion with long-time friend and full-Finn Eleanor Ostman, former food writer for the *St. Paul Pioneer Press*. Eleanor contributed her experience with writing recipes and self-publishing cookbooks, including *Always on Sunday* based on her 30-year Tested Recipes column in the Sunday *Pioneer Press*.

The "look" of this book was created by Sexton Printing's talented designer Kimberlea Weeks who made these pages sparkle.

Soile is deeply grateful to her international crew of kitchen leaders and chefs who were the soul of Deco Catering's cuisine for decades and directed a large staff of devoted cooks. They are, from left in front, Alexandra Awadeh, Nancy Muy and Farahnez Solimanpoor, with Anthony Lusian at the back. They continue their expertise at Deco under new ownership. She also thanks her catering leader Maiju Kontti, also a native of Finland, who for nearly 30 years has staged and overseen service at parties and events. "She is gifted with flowers and artistic food display while managing up to 60 people. She is the best! The captain of the boat!" says Soile, who also thanks the many other loyal catering leaders who took responsibility when multiple parties were on the schedule.

Heikki Rouvinen oversees Deco Catering's business and customer relations. Soile's right-hand man — and son — was trained in hospitality management in Leysin, Switzerland and the United States. Prior to joining Deco, Heikki worked for the family resort in Finland and UBS in Europe. "I am so lucky to have Heikki work with me for so long, growing the company for 14 years. It was a pleasure to have him by my side," says Soile. He continues at Deco as a part-owner and partner as the business continues to flourish.

the DECO CATERING

Deco Corporation was born when Soile opened the Deco Restaurant in 1982 in the Minnesota Museum of Art, St. Paul. Deco Catering was an outgrowth, operating in North Oaks and Minneapolis. She sold that business in 2015, and it continues under new ownership. For more information, go to www.decocatering.com.

TASTE of Scandinavia BAKERY & CAFÉ SINCE 1992

taste OF SCANDINAVIA bakery & café

Taste of Scandinavia, founded by Soile in 1992 and sold in 2004, continues as a successful business under the leadership of Lauri Youngquist, Owner, CEO and President of the bakery and cafe company, with several Twin Cities locations. For more information, go to www.tasteofscandinavia.com.

The Finnish Bistro

When Taste of Scandinavia was sold, Soile kept the Como Avenue location in St. Paul, renaming it in 2004 as The Finnish Bistro to reflect her native country. She sold the restaurant to its former manager Sandra Weise in 2013, and it continues to thrive. For more information go to www.finnishbistro.com.

"I am so happy that my ideas for businesses are still thriving, providing work for many, many people and pleasing so many customers." — Soile Anderson

A Mid-Summer Party for Martha Stewart's Magazine

Soile still doesn't know how entertaining guru Martha Stewart got her name, but there was her secretary on the phone, requesting preparation of a Scandinavian-style Midsummer dinner, cooked outdoors on the shores of a Minnesota lake. The resulting story, recipes and photos graced 12 pages of *Martha Stewart Living* magazine, June 2002.

No problem. In her native eastern Finland, Soile celebrated midsummer all her young years, eating traditional foods, dancing around bonfires until the sun nearly disappeared briefly during the wee hours, only to rise again early on the first day of the new season. All the cooking was done outdoors.

DINNER MENU

Lingonberry Punch

Blinis with Caviar and
Cucumber-Dill Dressing

Karjalan Potato Pies with
Egg Butter

Pickled Herring

Rye Sourdough Bread

Finnish Fish Soup

Hot Smoked Salmon Steaks
with Morel Mushroom Sauce

Baby Red Potatoes

Cucumber Salad

Cloudberry Cake

Lingonberry Punch

6 cups fresh lingonberries

**1.75 liter bottle good-quality vodka,
chilled**

**2 gallons lingonberry juice (available
at IKEA) or substitute cranberry juice**

Place lingonberries in a resealable
plastic storage bag and place in
the freezer until they are completely
frozen, at least two hours. Combine
vodka and juice in a large punch
bowl. Add frozen berries.
Serve immediately.

Makes 30 servings.

At her own lake home in North Oaks, Minnesota, she set waterside tables
with blue and white linens and dishes with yellow accents, echoing Finnish
and Swedish flag colors. Lanterns were centerpieces, lit when the sun finally
waned. Chilled vodka and lingonberry punch greeted guests, and, just as
in Finland, they dined on fish soup simmered in a huge cauldron over an
open fire. They savored blinis with caviar and Cucumber-Dill Dressing
(recipe on page 85). Hot smoked salmon dressed with morel sauce and
baby red potatoes were offered with cucumber salads. A traditional
Cloudberry Cake, flavored with the rare yellow cloudberries from the
Lapland region, ended the longest day's feast.

TIP | Freeze ferns and
lingonberries in the ice block.

Fabulous Finnish Fish Soup

10 cups fish stock (see directions below)

Soup:

2 cups chopped carrots

2 cups chopped onion

2 cups chopped celery

6 cups peeled and cubed potatoes

**1 tablespoon whole peppercorns
(if desired, use whole allspice)**

4 to 5 cups uncooked salmon, cubed

1 pint heavy cream

1 stick butter

1 cup chopped fresh dill

1/2 cup chopped chives

To make homemade fish stock, buy a whole salmon. Fillet, removing meat from skin and bones. Set meat aside, well wrapped, in refrigerator. In a large stockpot, place 3 quarts water. Add 2 roughly-chopped onions, a handful each of roughly chopped carrots and celery, 2 tablespoons pickling spice and a tablespoon of Kosher salt. Add salmon bones, skin and head plus 2 cloves of garlic. Simmer for 1-1/2 to 2 hours, tasting to see if it needs more salt. Strain stock, measuring 10 cups for the soup.

Place the 10 cups of stock into a large soup pot over medium heat. Chop the carrots, onion and celery, and prepare the potatoes. Cube 4 to 5 cups salmon for the soup; reserve the remaining salmon for other uses, freezing if necessary.

Add the chopped carrots, onion and celery to simmering broth; cook vegetables for about 10 minutes. Add the potatoes and peppercorns or allspice. Cook for about 20 minutes or until the potatoes become tender. Add the cubed salmon, heavy cream, butter, fresh dill and chives. Simmer for 10 to 15 minutes until salmon is opaque. Taste, adding salt if needed. Serve hot.

Makes 12 to 15 servings.

TIP | If you don't want to buy a whole salmon, ask your fish merchant to give you salmon bones, skin and head for the stock.

Finnish Blinis

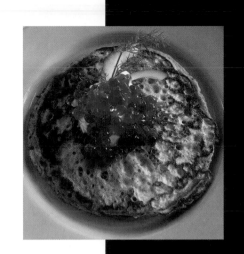

2 cups milk

1 ounce fresh yeast

1/2 cup buckwheat flour

3/4 cup all-purpose flour

3 tablespoons butter, melted

2 egg yolks

2 egg whites, beaten

1 teaspoon salt

Butter for frying

Heat milk gently so it is just warm. Stir in yeast. Mix in buckwheat and all-purpose flours. Allow mixture to rest in a warm place until the yeast has had a chance to work with the milk and flours, 1 to 2 hours, and the mixture bubbles and turns slightly sour. Then beat the butter into the egg yolks, and stir into the flour mixture Whisk the egg whites until stiff, and fold into the batter. Stir in salt.

Heat a 6-inch frying pan and melt butter in it. Spoon batter into the pan to form a 5-inch blini. (Can be made larger, if desired.) Fry, then flip to cook both sides. Repeat with remaining batter. Serve warm with Cucumber-Dill Dressing (recipe on page 85) and caviar.

Makes about 14 blinis.

Soile simmers Finnish Fish Soup in an impressive iron cauldron over a wood fire in her backyard.

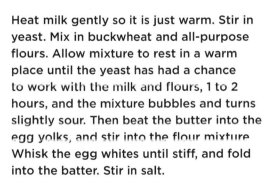

TIP | An iron cauldron over a wood fire adds ambiance to any outdoor party. Such kettles can be found at farm auctions. Preserve as you would a cast iron frying pan, seasoning with oil between uses.

TIP | The same technique for hot-smoking salmon steaks can be used to cook whole salmon fillets.

TIP | To make a salmon butterfly steak, cut an 8 ounce portion and then cut lengthwise through the meat and but not through the skin. Fold in half, skin side to the center.

Hot Smoked Salmon

2 cups natural wood chips

2-1/2 cups water

1 tablespoon sugar

Charcoal heated in the grill until red

Olive oil

Salmon butterfly steaks, 8 ounces each, seasoned with 1 teaspoon lemon pepper and 1/2 teaspoon salt per steak

Soak the wood chips in water-sugar mixture for 1 hour. Meanwhile, heat charcoal. Brush salmon steaks with oil and season with lemon pepper and salt. Brush grill rack with oil. Push hot coals to one side of the grill. Place wet chips on top of charcoal. Place salmon toward the center of the grill, away from direct heat. Cover grill. Make sure vent is open. Cook salmon for about 15 to 20 minutes. Serve salmon with Morel Mushroom Sauce or Cucumber-Dill Dressing (recipe on page 85), new potatoes with dill and roasted summer vegetables.

Allow one salmon steak per person.

Morel Sauce

1-1/2 sticks unsalted butter, divided

2 cups finely chopped yellow onions

4 cloves garlic, minced

2 pounds fresh morel mushrooms, coarsely chopped (cremini or chanterelles can be substituted)

Coarse salt and freshly ground pepper

1-1/2 cups dry white wine

1 cup homemade or low-sodium canned chicken stock

3 cups heavy cream

1/2 cup fresh dill, coarsely chopped

Melt 1/4 cup butter in a large skillet over medium heat. Add onions and garlic; sauté until onions are soft and translucent, about 10 minutes. Transfer to a bowl and set aside. In the same skillet, melt 1/2 cup butter. Add mushrooms and season with salt and pepper. Sauté until morels are soft and their released juices have reduced so they just cover the bottom of the pan, about 20 minutes. Return onion mixture to skillet. Add wine and cook until it has reduced by half, about 7 minutes. Add chicken stock and cream, stirring occasionally until liquid is bubbling and starts to thicken, 18 to 20 minutes. Remove from heat and stir in dill just before serving.

Makes 8 cups.

Cloudberry Cake

6 eggs

1/1/2 cups sugar

1 cup all-purpose flour

1 cup potato flour or cornstarch

1 teaspoon baking powder

Filling and frosting:

4 cups heavy cream

2 cups powdered sugar

5 cups cloudberry jam, divided (available at IKEA)

To make cake: Cream the eggs and sugar until fluffy. Combine the dry ingredients and add to the egg mixture; mix well. Grease a deep springform 12-inch round pan with removable bottom. Add batter and bake 35 to 45 minutes at 350 degrees. Test with toothpick for doneness. Cool the cake. Cut the cake horizontally into three layers.

To make filling and frosting: Whip cream until stiff and beat in powdered sugar. Place one cake layer on a serving plate. Spread with 1-1-/2 cups cloudberry jam and top that with whipped cream. Repeat the layers. Place remaining layer on top. Use remaining whipped cream to frost the cake. Pour remaining cloudberry jam over the top of cake allowing it to drip down the sides.

Optional: Raspberry jam or other fillings can be used in place of cloudberry jam.

Makes 16 servings.

Cloudberries are native to Northern Finland.

Cucumber Salad

16 cucumbers, peeled and thinly sliced

2 cups white wine vinegar

1 large bunch fresh dill, chopped fine (remove the larger stems first)

2 tablespoons coarse (Kosher) salt

3 tablespoons sugar

Combine all ingredients in a large bowl. Stir until sugar and salt are dissolved and cucumbers are evenly coated. Cover bowl with plastic wrap and store in refrigerator for at least 1 hour before serving. Salad can be kept in an airtight container in refrigerator for up to 3 days.

Makes 20 to 25 servings.

A Rabbi's Guide to Kosher Celebrations

Marcia Zimmerman, Senior Rabbi at Temple Israel, Minneapolis, has played the Bar and Bat Mitzvah hat trick. She had her own Bat Mitzvah ceremony at 24. Her three children have reached the age of maturity through the traditional ceremonies so she's hosted parties, and as a Rabbi, she oversees the celebrations in the entire congregation. Because she was Rabbi as well as mother, "we had to invite the entire congregation for my kids' parties," she says. "We fed over 600 people kugel and tuna salad," she said of her oldest daughter's event. Her second daughter had specific food preferences, so pesto yes, tuna no.

"When my youngest child came along, I got an anonymous letter from someone in the congregation, who suggested we stick to a traditional meal," she recalls. "But we mixed it up a little bit."

"Bar" means son, of age at 13 and one day; "bat" means daughter, ready at 12 years 6 months. The congregation celebrates a child's transition to adulthood with a ceremony which demonstrates the Jewish tradition appreciates kids and families. Young people looking toward their Bar/Bat Mitzvah ceremony learn Hebrew while preparing themselves to prove to the congregation that they are ready to take on the responsibilities and leadership of the Jewish faith.

"Parties can get overblown," Rabbi Zimmerman concedes. "After all, they're for someone who's just 12 or 13." The event, with all its décor and elaborate fare, is considered a reward for the efforts of study, "but really, the party celebrates Judaism. It comes at a time in life that may be difficult for any young person. In Jewish belief, this life cycle event brings family and friends together before separation into adulthood and the next doorways of life," said the Rabbi. "We celebrate you. And then let you go, launching you for what's to come."

Rabbi Zimmerman recalls the trend to really lavish parties began in the 1980s when times were good. The economic downturn of 2008 caused some families to temper their celebrations, but more recently, big bashes are back.

The service itself, with all the pressure on the young person, "is an anthropologic near-death experience, one that must be survived," the Rabbi said.

Take a deep breath. Perform well. Because after all that effort, there's food and fun.

A vibrant challah cover over the bread is removed upon the Rabbi's blessing. Such covers are passed from generation to generation.

 Symbol indicates Kosher Celebrations within this book.

Chocolate Marshmallow Bars

This is the Kaplan family's favorite dessert, which was served at their son's Bar Mitzvah and at every family gathering.

2/3 cup butter

1 package (12 ounces) semi-sweet chocolate chips

1 cup sugar

1 teaspoon salt

2 teaspoons vanilla

4 eggs

1-1/2 cups flour

Glaze:

1-1/2 cups semi-sweet chocolate chips

2 tablespoons butter

1/4 cup Karo syrup

1 jar marshmallow creme

To make the bars: Melt butter and chips in a pan over low heat. Remove from heat. Blend in sugar, salt and vanilla. Add eggs one at a time, beating after each addition. Add flour. Spread in a greased 9-by-13-inch pan. Bake at 350 degrees for 20 to 25 minutes.

To make the glaze: While bars are baking, combine chocolate chips, butter and Karo syrup. Melt over low heat or in the microwave oven. When bars are removed from the oven, spoon on marshmallow creme and return to the oven for a few seconds to soften. Remove from the oven and spread the marshmallow creme evenly. Then drizzle the chocolate mixture over the marshmallow layer. Cool, then freeze until firm. When ready to serve, thaw and cut into squares. Refrigerate any leftover bars.

Makes 30 servings.

Sue Kaplan Remembers:

When our son's Bar Mitzvah was approaching I was hoping to find a caterer who could "Think Outside the Box." I had been to several wonderful events and the name Soile Anderson kept popping up when I inquired about the caterer. We wanted to have our Bar Mitzvah luncheon at our conservative Temple. That was a problem because Soile was not a certified Kosher caterer. I decided to take a chance and ask her if she'd be willing to meet with me and my Rabbi to discuss the possibility of becoming certified. She agreed, and then it began. With enthusiasm, she went though a rigorous course and was ready for her first Kosher catering at our son's Bar Mitzvah. Soile and her dedicated staff pulled out all the stops. The quality of the food and her creative presentation were outstanding, and from there her Kosher catering business took off.

Kaplan explained that at a Mitzvah, "it is traditional for Jewish adults to wear a Tallit (prayer shawl). A total of 613 knotted fringes on the Tallit serve as a reminder of God's 613 commandments. As part of the Bar or Bat Mitzvah ceremony, a Tallit and yarmulke are presented to the son or daughter by the parents." The photos show the Kaplan family's Tallit that had been passed forward over generations. A boy's shawl has blue stripes; a girl wears one with lovely symbolic embroidery on the shawl and on the bag in which it is stored.

TRADITION, TRADITION!

Friday Night Formal Family Dinner

That stirring song from "Fiddler on the Roof" describes the Friday night gathering for the Bar or Bat Mitzvah honoree and family, when foods are traditional and good wishes are sincere. Challah, wine and glowing candles are blessed and matzah ball soup is a must.

But tradition can be tweaked a bit, and Soile made the foods lively if the family agreed to be adventuresome. Loaves of challah, freshly-baked before sunset, center the tables, so everyone can "break bread." It can be from a classic recipe or enriched with eggs or honey. Or as an ode to her Scandinavian heritage, it is often flavored with cardamom.

Matzah Ball Soup — oh, the ways it can be nuanced! Soile's first soup attempts were a challenge. "It didn't taste quite right, but then a 103-year-old Jewish woman known as Grandma Ruth taught me her soup tricks, and we found perfection." Eaten with fresh challah, the soup is a warming and wonderful first course.

For hosts seeking "something different," Soile might prepare stuffed Kosher chicken breasts with spinach, mushrooms, sun-dried tomatoes, onion and a hint of garlic. Or suggest a brisket bathed in barbecue sauce. As long as Kosher rules are followed, anything is possible.

But on Friday night, she advises to "keep it simple."

Matzah Ball Soup

Challah Bread

Salad Course

Herbal Roasted-on-the-Bone Chicken Quarters,
Stuffed Chicken or Chicken Roll-Ups

Barbecued Beef Brisket or Roasted Brisket

Roasted Salmon

Lamb-Stuffed Eggplant

Roasted Vegetables and Potatoes

Flourless Chocolate Cake with Raspberry Sauce,
Meringues with Fruit and Chocolate Sauce or Fruit Sorbets

Passover Popovers

1-1/2 cups water

1/2 cup vegetable oil

3/4 cup matzah cake meal

3/4 cup matzah meal

6 eggs

In a saucepan, bring water and oil to a boil. Mix the matzah cake meal and matzah meal together; stir into water-oil mixture, mixing well. Remove from heat. Add the eggs one at a time, beating well after each addition. Grease 12 muffin cups. Fill cups half full with batter. Bake at 400 degrees for 40 to 50 minutes until puffed and browned. Serve immediately.

Makes 12 popovers.

Friday night dinner in her home was hosted by Melanie Berry.

Celebration Chicken Soup

1 whole chicken (older, larger bird)

2 brown-skinned yellow onions (leave skin on)

1-1/2 tablespoons sugar

1/2 to 1 tablespoon salt, to taste

1 to 1-1/2 teaspoons pepper, to taste

5 carrots, pared and julienned

2 stalks celery, trimmed and julienned

1 bunch parsley, chopped

1 bunch fresh dill, chopped

Place the cleaned chicken into a large pot full of cold water. Place on heat. When the water comes to a boil, skim fat from surface. After skimming, add uncut, skin-on onions, sugar, salt and pepper, adjusting for taste. Cover pot, but leave cover slightly ajar; turn heat down and simmer for about an hour or more. Remove chicken and strain the broth through a colander.

Divide broth into two pots. In one pot, simmer matzah balls until they rise to the surface. To the other half of the broth, add julienned carrots and celery. Simmer for 30 minutes. Taste broth for seasonings, adding more if necessary. Combine cooked matzah balls and broth with carrot-celery broth. Add dill and parsley. For each serving, ladle broth through bowl and add two matzah balls.

Note: If desired, chicken meat can be added to the soup.

Makes 16 to 24 servings.

Milk Meal Options | Some families prefer a milk-based meal. They might choose Carrot Ginger or Butternut Squash or Tomato Basil soup, Greek Salad with Feta Cheese or Tomato Mozzarella Salad, Roasted Salmon Steak or Individual Salmon Wellingtons with Roasted New Potatoes and Seasonal Vegetables topped with Dill Dressing. A cheese and vegetable lasagna is another option, or an Italian Torta layering vegetables, cheeses and sour cream pastry dough.

TIP | Use flowers for the Friday dinner that can be reused on Saturday in different arrangements.

Grandma Ruth's Matzah Balls

4 eggs, separated

1/2 teaspoon salt plus extra salt to flavor the cooking water

1/4 teaspoon pepper

Matzah Meal (1 cup, plus more as needed)

Fill a large pot or Dutch oven almost full with water. Add salt to the water (at least one teaspoon). Place over medium heat to start it boiling.

To make the matzah balls: Separate egg yolks and whites in two bowls. Beat the whites into stiff peaks. Add salt and pepper. Beat the egg yolks. Fold the yolks into the whites. Gradually add matzah meal by folding it gently into the egg mixture until it reaches a texture that can be formed into balls. Add more matzah if needed, but do not make the mixture overly thick.

Fill a bowl with ice water for dipping hands before forming balls. Form mixture into golf ball-sized balls. Drop each ball into boiling water as it is formed. Dip hands into ice water if they get sticky. When all the balls are in the water, adjust heat so it is boiling at a moderate rate. Cook the balls for about 25 minutes. Cover the pot as the balls cook, but leave cover ajar so steam can escape.

Remove matzah balls with a slotted spoon. Serve immediately or refrigerate overnight.

Makes 6 matzah balls. Multiply recipe according to the number of soup servings.

Green salad with fresh berries — no cheese — is best with a simple herbal vinaigrette.

Chicken breast stuffed with spinach, onions and mushrooms is served with mango salsa.

Savory Beef Brisket

1 beef brisket, 3 to 4 pounds

Salt and pepper

3/4 cup brown sugar

1 teaspoon cayenne pepper

Cabbage leaves

2 onions, thinly sliced

2 carrots, thinly sliced

1 stalk celery, thinly sliced

1 whole head of garlic, peeled and crushed

Approximately 1 quart pineapple juice

1 bottle (12 ounces) tomato-based chili sauce

Roasted chicken quarters.

Preheat the oven to 325 degrees. Season the brisket with salt and a generous amount of black pepper. Rub with a mixture of brown sugar and cayenne pepper. Line a roasting pan with cabbage leaves. Add the brisket to the pan and brown in the oven for about 1 hour. Remove from oven. Cover with a layer of sliced onions and top with carrots, celery and garlic. Mix together pineapple juice and chili sauce; pour over brisket. Cover baking pan with parchment paper and tin foil. Return to oven and bake about 3-1/2 hours. Slice and serve with brisket with roasted vegetables. Just before serving, strain pan liquids and pour over meat.

Makes 12 to 15 servings.

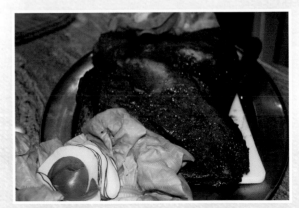

Savory beef brisket.

Flourless chocolate cake served with fresh raspberry puree.

Lamb-Stuffed Eggplant

2 eggplants

1/2 cup olive oil

1 pound ground lamb

1 tablespoon chopped garlic

1/2 cup chopped onion

1 cup sliced porcini or button mushrooms

1 tomato, cubed

1/2 cup chopped red pepper

1/2 cup chopped Italian parsley

Salt and pepper

Filling: Cut eggplants in half and remove centers to create serving bowls, reserving removed eggplant. In a sauté pan with 1/2 cup olive oil, brown the lamb. Remove the lamb to a bowl, leaving the oil-drippings in the pan. Add reserved eggplant, garlic, onion and mushrooms; sauté until softened. Add sautéed lamb, tomato, red pepper and parsley; mix well and season to taste.

To prepare eggplant bowls: Sauté bowls in additional olive oil, cut side down, until browned. Fill the bowls with the lamb mixture. Bake at 350 degrees for 45 minutes. Serve with lingonberry sauce.

Serves 4 — half eggplant each.

Flourless Chocolate Dessert

1 pound Kosher dark chocolate

1/2 pound Kosher margarine
(or butter if cakes are served with dairy meal)

1/4 cup sugar

8 eggs

1/4 cup strong coffee

Melt chocolate and butter together in top of a double boiler. Beat sugar and eggs together in a separate bowl. Cool chocolate mixture slightly so eggs, added slowly, don't scramble. Stir in coffee. Put paper liners into muffin cups to make about 24 cakes. Spoon mixture into pans. Place muffin pans in a larger deep baking pan. Add 1/2 inch of water into deep baking pan. Bake at 325 degrees for 20 to 25 minutes.

To glaze individual cakes: Freeze individual cakes with paper liners. Melt 1 pound coating chocolate in top of double boiler. Remove paper liners and dip cakes one at a time into chocolate and place on rack to allow coating to drip.

Raspberry sauce: Blend 6 cups of frozen raspberries with 2 cups of sugar until pureed. If desired, add 1 tablespoons of Sabra liqueur.

Makes 24 servings.

Salmon Wellington

Pastry:

1 recipe sour cream dough (see page 50)

Filling for 2 individual servings:

2 tablespoons butter

1/2 cup finely chopped onion

1/2 cup sliced mushrooms (any variety)

1 cup sautéed spinach

1 tablespoon chopped red pepper

1 tablespoon chopped yellow pepper

2 tablespoons feta cheese

1 teaspoon Paul Prudhomme Vegetable Magic seasoning

Salt to taste

Wellington assembly:

2 pieces (6 ounces each) salmon fillet, skin removed

1 tablespoon lemon pepper

1 egg, beaten

Ellyn Wolfenson Remembers:

I first heard about Soile over twenty five years ago. Her food was described to me as delicious and well displayed. I figured, great, I entertain a lot, was a young mother of four children under ten at that time and thought I would hand the reins over to a professional for a party my husband and I were hosting. Whoooahhh, little did I know that not only would I be providing my guests with the most delicious food they had ever tasted, but in addition, it would be a breathtaking display of art at the same time. Soile literally transformed my kitchen into a gorgeous garden eminating from my own center island! The fruit was cascading beautifully, the stove was covered with leaves and crabapple branches, and the actual food display was not to be believed. To say it was delicious, is one of the universe's greatest understatements! Twenty-five years, several family, life cycle, civic and community events later, Soile's Salmon Wellington with cucumber sauce is still my "go to" main course! Now those four children under ten are grown adults hosting their own personal and civic events and who is their first call? ....Yup, SOILE.

Sauté onion and mushrooms lightly in butter. Add spinach and continue to sauté until softened. Cool slightly and drain very well, pressing out excess moisture. Add red and yellow peppers and feta. Add Vegetable Magic and salt to taste.

Sprinkle salmon pieces with lemon pepper. Roll out the sour cream dough in one large piece. Divide filling mixture into two mounds on one end of dough. Top with salmon fillets. Cut dough in half between salmon. Starting at the top, roll salmon with dough, tucking ends and sides under to make a smooth package. Use scraps of dough to decorate Wellingtons. Brush with egg. Bake Wellingtons at 350 degrees for about 45 minutes or until golden brown. Serve with dill sour cream sauce. Makes 2 servings.

For a whole salmon fillet, remove skin. Quadruple the filling recipe, then follow instructions, placing filling in one mound and topping with salmon before covering with dough. Bake at 350 degrees for 45 minutes to an hour.

Whole salmon fillet makes 6 to 8 servings.

Salmon Wellington made with the whole salmon fillet. Serves 6 to 8.

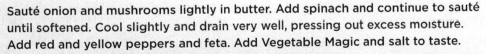

21

Kugel, Bagels — Luncheons to Love

Poached pear salad with cranberries, walnuts, and Roquefort cheese. See tip on page 93.

Lox salmon platter, recipe on page 68.

Quinoa salad, recipe on page 89.

Blow-out Saturday Celebrations

Oh, the relief! The service is over, the questions have been answered, and the young person has passed into adulthood. Let's eat!

Saturday buffet lunches are typically milk meals, and certain favorites are essential and anticipated by the crowd that can number several hundred. Fresh bagels in assorted flavors are slathered with cream cheese, but some families also asked Soile's team to bake homemade mixed-berry or spinach scones. Baguettes are also popular, perhaps spread with hummus.

Herbal-roasted salmon is an option to lox platters.

Everyone loves to spoon into hot kugel, offered with sour cream and jam, but they might also add quiche to their plates. Salads according to the season — at least three kinds — add color and crunch. Soile's own recipe for lox is popular with her clients, especially paired with bagels and cream cheese, but another option is oven-roasted salmon with dill sauce. For a no-meat lunch, some hosts order vegetable casseroles, crepes filled with fruit or vegetable mixtures, perhaps vegetarian moussaka or lasagna.

Everyone saves room for a lavish buffet of sweets.

Centerpieces are typically seasonal fruits or flowers, and the buffet has "that layered look" with foodstuffs displayed on several levels. "It's important to give guests a 'Wow!' experience," Soile says.

Herbal roasted salmon platter. To prepare, brush salmon with olive oil and sprinkle lemon pepper and salt. Roast at 350 degrees for 20 minutes.

Savory Spinach and Cheese Scones

14 cups (4 pounds) flour

2-1/2 cups (1 pound) sugar

4 tablespoons baking powder

1-1/2 pounds butter, at room temperature

14 eggs

4-1/2 cups buttermilk

2-1/2 pounds fresh spinach, finely chopped

1-1/2 pounds (6 cups) shredded mozzarella cheese

2 to 3 tablespoons Paul Prudhomme Vegetable Magic seasoning (optional)

Egg wash

Combine flour, sugar and baking powder in a large mixer bowl. Add butter and mix with a paddle attachment until fine crumbs form. Whip eggs in a separate bowl. Add buttermilk. In a very large bowl, combine flour and egg mixtures together with gloved hands. Add chopped spinach, cheese and seasoning. Place 3-ounce scoops of the mixture on sprayed parchment paper-lined pans. Beat egg and use to glaze scones. Place in 350-degree oven for 26 minutes.

Or unbaked scones can be frozen and then placed in plastic storage bags and frozen for future use, using egg wash just before baking from a frozen state. Bake at 350 degrees for 30 to 35 minutes till lightly golden. No need to thaw first.

Fresh blueberries can be used instead of spinach.

Makes 48 scones.

TYPICAL SATURDAY LUNCHEON BUFFET MENU

Bagels, Scones, French Bread

Cream Cheese and Butter

Lox Salmon Platter with Dilled Sour Cream

Hummus and Baba Ganoush

Egg Salad and Tuna Salad

Tomato Cucumber Salad

Couscous or Quinoa Salads

Green Salad with Poached Pears

Marinated Green Beans with Mushrooms

Spinach or Vegetarian Quiche

Italian Torta

Stuffed Rainbow Trout or Roasted Salmon

Kugel

Crepes with Jam or Berries and Cream

Baked Brie with Fruit

Kids prefer:

Macaroni and Cheese

Tomato Basil Soup

Grilled Cheese Sandwiches

Calzone or Pizza

Fruit Salad

Kugel

2 pounds egg noodles

1 stick butter, melted

2 quarts (64 ounces) buttermilk

8 eggs, beaten

1 cup sugar

1/2 teaspoon Kosher salt

Topping:

2-1/4 cups brown sugar

2 cups corn flake crumbs

1 stick butter, melted

Cook noodles, then drain them. Place noodles in a buttered 10-by-20-inch pan. Drizzle 1/4 pound melted butter over the noodles. Combine buttermilk, beaten eggs, sugar and salt; blend well and pour over the noodles. For the topping, mix brown sugar, corn flake crumbs and remaining butter. Sprinkle over noodles.

Bake for 1 hour at 350 degrees.

Makes 24 servings.

Think Spring

After a legendary Minnesota winter, the Bat Mitzvah hosts wanted, through food and decor, to create a warm sunny springtime atmosphere.

The golden brilliance of forsythia towered over a table ripe with succulent fruits and spring flavors including broccoli with herbal sour cream dressing, marinated cucumber salad, couscous, quinoa with tomatoes and feta, and asparagus tossed with raspberry vinaigrette. Herbed focaccia bread added lively crunch.

Rainbow desserts featuring springtime colors and flavors illustrate Soile's commitment to fresh and homemade. "At Deco, we always baked from scratch — no mixes," she says. Old-style, good quality desserts are so important to making clients and guests pleased. "People always remember beautiful, hand-crafted treats."

Scandinavian Raspberry Torte

Scandinavian Sandbakkels

24

Soile's Favorite Sandwich Cookie

2-1/2 pounds butter

2 cups sugar

5 egg yolks

3-1/2 pounds flour

Filling:

Apricot jam

Glaze:

3 cups powdered sugar

Juice from thawed frozen raspberries

To make the cookie dough, cream butter and sugar in an electric mixer using a paddle attachment. Add egg yolks and mix well. Add flour and beat until blended. Roll out the dough on a floured surface. Cut with a 1-7/8-inch round cutter. Place on ungreased sheet pans lined with parchment paper. Bake at 350 degrees for 10 to 12 minutes, until edges are golden brown. Remove from the oven and cool on parchment paper.

To fill: Lightly spread half of the cookies with apricot jam. Top each one with another cookie.

To glaze: Stir raspberry juice into powdered sugar, using enough of the juice to make a glaze that is spreadable but not too thick. Spread glaze on sandwich cookies.

Makes about 125 sandwich cookies. If desired, the cookies can be baked ahead of time and frozen, then filled and glazed just before serving.

Pastel Pretty

Ruthie Posada prefers pastel colors. She likes hats. And she likes cats.

Soile used those hints to create Ruthie's Bat Mitzvah party for 175 guests.

Table décor centered on a rainbow of pastel balloons, tablecloths and napkins, contrasted by crisp white chair covers.

Fortunately, Ruthie didn't insist on pastel food. Shown right is a colorful table of fruits and salads, including an Italian-style Caprese blend of tomatoes, basil and miniature Mozzarella balls. She also wanted a pizza bar for her young friends to savor.

Ruthie, above all, wanted her friends to have fun, so her party was outfitted with games — basketball free-throw challenges, Foosball, and other tests of skill.

Guests entered the party under an arch of ribbon-bedecked balloons — in pastel colors, of course.

Ruthie also chose the melting intenseness of a deeply-chocolate Lava Cake.

TIP | Balloons anchored with foil-wrapped weights decorated tables. Chocolate treats completed the centerpieces.

MEDITERRANEAN MENU

Veggie Chips and Dips

Couscous

Fruit Salads

Pita Bread

Baba Ganoush

Hummus

Caprese Salad

Garbanzo Bean Salad
with Vegetables

Lentil Salad

Mediterranean
Vegetable Torta

Lava Cake

Those who shared Ruthie's love of cats could make a fluffy cat toy using squares of fleece and a cord to dangle it. Sure to fascinate a feline.

At left, brilliant hats were available for those who wanted to don colorful chapeaus when they visited the photo booth. Ruthie models her choice.

At right, one of the several games guest enjoyed.

Lava Cake and ice cream-filled Almond Cookie Basket garnished with fresh berries.

TIP | Drizzle raspberry puree (recipe on page 20) and chocolate sauce on the plate to underscore the desserts.

Lava Cake

1 stick firm butter

4 ounces chocolate chips, semi-sweet or bittersweet (2/3 of a small bag)

1 cup powdered sugar

2 eggs, beaten

2 egg yolks, beaten

1 teaspoon instant coffee powder (optional)

1 teaspoon vanilla

1/3 cup flour

1/2 teaspoon salt

Place muffin cup liners in medium-sized muffin tin. Coat papers with baking spray. Melt butter and chocolate chips in a medium-sized glass bowl in the microwave or in the top of a double boiler, stirring to blend. Stir in powdered sugar. Stir in the eggs and extra yolks, the coffee powder and vanilla. Add flour and salt, combining well. Spoon mixture into lined muffin cups, filling quite full. Bake at 400 degrees for 12 minutes, until the sides are set but the centers are still soft. Remove from the oven and cool muffin pan on a rack for about 5 minutes. Invert cakes on serving plates, pulling off paper liners.

To frost:

Combine 1 cup sweetened condensed milk, a dash of salt, 1 cup semi-sweet chocolate chips and 1/4 teaspoon vanilla in sauté pan. Heat, stirring constantly, until chocolate melts and mixture thickens. Remove from heat, then spoon over Lava Cakes. Dust with powdered sugar before serving with ice-cream-filled Almond Spoon Cookies.

Makes 6 servings.

Almond Cookie Basket

Recipe courtesy of Sharon Severson.

7 tablespoons soft butter

Scant cup of ground unblanched almonds

3/4 cup white sugar

1 tablespoon flour

2 tablespoons heavy cream

1/4 teaspoon vanilla

Melt butter in a saucepan. Stir in ground almonds, sugar, flour, cream and vanilla. Blend well. Using parchment paper on a cookie sheet, drop the mixture by teaspoons three inches apart. Bake at 375 degrees for 5 to 7 minutes, until edges begin to brown but centers are still bubbling. Cool slightly for about 45 seconds. With a wide thin spatula, drape the cookies over the bottom of coffee cups. Cool.

To serve. Fill each cup with a scoop of ice cream and garnish with fresh fruit and a mint leaf.

Makes 6 cookie baskets.

TIP | Have some immediately-available healthy snacks and dips for always-hungry young guests. Here we see sweet potato and zucchini chips plus a toss of julienned raw vegetable sticks served with salsa and avocado dips (recipes on page 56 and 57).

Veggie Chips

Your choice of pared zucchini, sweet potato, red beets or potatoes

Rice wine vinegar

Olive oil

Paul Prudhomme Vegetable Magic seasoning or salt and pepper

Using a mandolin, thinly slice your choice of vegetables. Combine equal parts of rice wine vinegar and olive oil in amounts adequate for the volume of vegetables. Brush vegetable slices with the vinegar-oil mixture, and place on baking sheets lined with parchment paper. Sprinkle with Vegetable Magic or salt and pepper. Roast in a 400-degree oven until lightly browned. Dry chips on paper towels to absorb any extra oil. Place clean parchment paper on pans; spread chips on pans. Turn off heat and place pans in slowly-cooling oven until chips are crispy.

Jacy's Springtime Bat Mitzvah

TIP | Jacy's favorite watermelon salad: cubed seedless watermelon (yellow and red), diced feta cheese, fresh mint with salt and pepper make a refreshing springtime flavor.

Planned months ahead, an Earth Day Bat Mitzvah theme spoke of springtime, but who knew if Minnesota weather in April would cooperate? As it turned out, the day was warm and sunny, but just to be safe, spring was brought indoors, with masses of flowers, white trellises and wicker picnic baskets overflowing with salads. Glass bowls fitted into the baskets kept everything tidy and allowed space for fresh garnishes. Tomato-basil-mozzarella salad, Scandinavian cucumber salad, tuna salad, Minnesota wild rice salad with smoked rainbow trout, watermelon salad with

feta cheese, and sugar-snap peas with spring vegetables and lemon vinaigrette were among the menu choices — all welcoming the coming summer season.

Whole poached salmon, decorated with cucumbers, lemon and dill, was the glamorous main course, accompanied with spinach quiche. Warm crepes filled with berries and whipped cream continued the colorful salute to spring. Nothing was complicated to prepare — but everything delivered on flavor and eye appeal.

Wendy Rubin's Spinach and Egg Bake

Jacy's mother's favorite egg dish

3 tablespoons oil

2 onions, chopped

2 packages (10 ounces each) frozen spinach, thawed and drained

10 eggs, beaten

1-1/2 pounds shredded Cheddar and Monterey Jack cheeses

1/4 teaspoon ground black pepper

Grease a 9-by-13-inch pan. Preheat oven to 350 degrees. Heat oil in large skillet and sauté onion until translucent, then add spinach, stirring well for a few minutes. Add eggs and cheese and mix well. Pour into pan and bake 45 to 50 minutes, until done in center. Cut into squares large or small — depending if it is main course or side dish. An easy gluten-free and crustless dish that can be made ahead.

Makes 15 to 20 servings.

TIP | To poach a whole cleaned salmon, place in a long poaching pan. Place whole peeled onions inside the cavity of the salmon to support it. Place whole carrots, cabbage quarters and celery chunks around the salmon. Season with salt and sprinkle with pickling spices. Add enough water to cover salmon. Cover the pan. Simmer slowly for 30 to 45 minutes, or until salmon is firm. Drain liquid (which can be saved to use when making fish soup). When salmon is cool, carefully remove the skin. Decorate as shown.

The honoree had her name spelled out in challah bread made by family friend Sandy Loewenstein.

Think Pink

Maggie wanted everything to be
pretty and pink for her Bat Mitzvah at
St. Paul's Temple of Aaron.
Sweet, too, with cookies, cakes and
candy a menu highlight.

Soile's grandson Nicklas, curious about the parties
she stages, came along for the event's set-up,
and when he saw all the goodies,
"he wanted to be Jewish, too!" she said.
"In the Finnish culture, we don't have such parties,
and Nicklas wondered why not?
He thought the party was the coolest thing,"
said grandma Soile. Even though he's a boy, and the decor
was girlish pink, he was convinced that he'd
enjoy being the guest of honor.

One stroke of luck — the dining chairs
at the temple were pink.

*Adults enjoyed "bouquets" with salad and fruit tucked into
Napa cabbage leaves, tied with red onion rings. Afterward,
they went to a pasta bar. Centering tables were floral
arrangements matching Maggie's pink theme.*

*Adults also indulged in chocolate and vanilla cupcakes topped
with pink whipped cream and an edible orchid.*

Should anyone forget whose party it was, MAGGIE was spelled out in pink letters, propped against the stage.

Typically at a mitzvah party, the honoree and young teen guests eat separately from adults. At the kids' tables were pink placemats tied with ribbon. When unwrapped, each guest found a bagel with tuna salad, pink cups of fresh fruit and vegetables with dip, and pink apricot sandwich cookie.

Every table had a tempting platter of pink candies played against chocolate varieties.

Soile's grandson, Nicklas, curious about catered mitzvah parties, helped make placemat packages with Grandma, left, and catering manager Toni Wilwerding.

SASHA'S BIG TOP

TRAPEZE

DRINKS

TIGHT ROPE

PHOTO BOOTH

SILKS & HOOPS

JUGGLING

Wow! Energetic kids were excited to the max when they arrived at Sasha Hausman's Big Top Bat Mitzvah. They could jump and climb and bounce and fly on circus equipment — when they weren't visiting the photo booth or walking a tight rope.

Held at a youth-oriented circus center, Circus Juventas, modeled after Cirque du Soleil, in St. Paul's Highland Park area, the play equipment and mats were already in place. Soile and her crew added the colorful pizazz. A riot of colors on tables and brilliant balloon art created a dazzling party scene. Fool-the-eye food amazed guests, young and older.

"Won't they melt?" everyone wondered when they saw a display of what they thought were ice cones. No worries! In white paper cups were cupcakes sprinkled with a rainbow of colored sugars. Spoons stuck into the cones were just for illusion. For energy, guests could load up at the appetizer table featuring flat breads with dips including hummus and baba ganoush.

An even closer view of the cupcake "cones" shows the intensity of colored sugars on the unmeltable dessert. The pompoms were made with carnations stuck in Styrofoam balls. For the Friday night dinner, the pompoms were individually placed on tables as centerpieces, then reused at the Saturday night circus party.

Hummus and eggplant dips are ready-to-spread on flatbread and pita.

MENU

Passed Appetizers

Flatbread Pizzas

Cheese Puff Pastry on a Stick

Seared Tuna with Wasabi
on Wonton Skins

Buffet

Roasted Eggplant Spread

Hummus and Baba Ganoush

Pita and European Breads

Orzo Salad with Pesto

Greek Quinoa Salad

New Potatoes with Onions and Capers

Southwest Black Bean Salad

Roasted Seasonal Vegetables

Herbal Roasted Wild Salmon Fillets
with Cucumber-Dill Dressing

Mac and Cheese for the Kids

Desserts

Popcorn Cupcakes

"Ice Cone" Cupcakes

Who ever heard of popcorn cupcakes? Not popcorn, but snipped miniature marshmallows created the topping for chocolate cupcakes.

Cocoa Cupcakes

2-1/4 cups all-purpose flour	1 cup vegetable oil
1 cup unsweetened cocoa powder	1 cup coffee liqueur or Kahlua
1-1/2 teaspoons baking soda	8 ounces sour cream
1 teaspoon baking powder	1 teaspoon pure vanilla
1/2 teaspoon salt	
2 cups sugar	
3 large eggs	

Sift together flour, cocoa, baking soda, baking power and salt. In large mixer, beat sugar and eggs until fluffy. Add oil, coffee liqueur, sour cream and vanilla; beat until smooth. Add flour mixture about a third at a time and beat after each addition until well-mixed and smooth. Spoon batter into cupcake pans lined with paper cups. Bake at 350 degrees for 20 to 25 minutes. After cupcakes are cooled, take out the center of each one using an apple corer. Fill the centers with chocolate mousse, heaping slightly.

Makes 24 or more cupcakes.

Chocolate Mousse Filling:

9 cups chocolate chips	3/4 cup Grand Marnier liqueur
1-1/2 pounds butter	2 cups egg whites
15 egg yolks	1/2 cup powdered sugar

This makes a large batch; freeze extra after filling cup cakes for future use with layer cakes, desserts, etc. To make mousse, melt chocolate chips in the top of a double boiler. Melt butter in a saucepan. In a large bowl, mix egg yolks and liqueur. When the chocolate is melted, remove from the double boiler. Place the bowl with the eggs on the bottom of the double boiler. Turn down heat so the water is at a medium boil. Cook the eggs, whisking until they are a creamy consistency. Do Not Allow to Curdle!

Remove eggs from heat and slowly whisk in hot butter. Add the melted chocolate in three stages, fully mixing after each addition. Whip the egg whites and powdered sugar until medium peaks form. Fold egg whites into chocolate mixture in three stages until well blended. Cover bowl and refrigerate until mousse becomes firm. Use to fill cupcakes or other cakes. Excess freezes well.

TIP | You can make a stand for the cupcake "cones" by drilling holes into plywood or metal and painting the display piece.

TENNIS EVERYONE?

When it comes to detail, Soile never misses the ball.

At the tennis-themed party, rather than just have a basket of rolls on the table, Soile and her baker fashioned tennis rackets out of French bread dough, complete with handle and stringing. The butter balls were miniature tennis balls. It was almost too amazing to tear apart and eat!

The table settings were a full-court press, with tennis balls, wrist cuffs, nets, lawn-tennis green grass on the tables and matching napkins tucked into goblets at each place setting.

The main course was individual Salmon Wellingtons (recipe on page 21) decorated with tennis rackets and balls using the same sour cream dough (recipe on page 50).

Dessert, shown on the tables and in more detail at right, featured cupcakes filled with chocolate mousse (recipe on page 37), topped with "tennis whites" whipped cream frosting, and a tennis ball formed from butter cream frosting and piped with chocolate to emulate an actual ball. Alongside is a tennis racket made with gingerbread cookie dough — notice the W for Wilson on the handle — decorated with white icing to form the netting. Underneath is coconut dyed grass green.

Soile gives kudos to ultra-creative party coordinator Lisa Kaplan and also to Richfield Flowers for smashing ambiance.

Imagine the cheers when these cupcakes were served!

Baskets of strawberries were studded with mini tennis balls made from yellow-dyed white chocolate, striped with dark chocolate.

TIP | From sturdy paper cut a miniature tennis racquet pattern to guide a sharp knife when cutting ginger cookie dough. Cool cookies before decorating with icing.

Ginger Cookies

2 sticks softened butter

1-1/2 cups sugar

1 egg

2 tablespoons dark corn syrup

1 tablespoon water

3-1/2 cups flour

2 teaspoons baking soda

1 teaspoon cinnamon

1 teaspoon ground ginger

1/2 teaspoon ground cloves

In a large bowl, cream the butter and sugar together. Add the egg and beat until light. Stir in the syrup and water. Combine the flour with soda, cinnamon, ginger and cloves. Stir into the creamed mixture until a dough forms. Gather into a ball.

Preheat oven to 325 degrees. Lightly grease baking sheets. Turn the dough onto a lightly-floured surface and roll out to about 1/4 inch thickness. Cut into desired shapes (for the tennis theme party, cookies were shaped like tennis rackets). Place on prepared cookie sheets; bake for 8 to 10 minutes or until set but not too brown. Cool on cookie sheets. Decorate with powdered sugar frosting.

Makes about 5 dozen cookies.

Valentine's Day

Sometimes, the date of a party can dictate decor.

Hearts and flowers were the theme for a Valentine's Day Bat Mitzvah which 200 guests absolutely loved, but the same ideas could be adapted to an engagement party or a romantic evening for two. Red table linen and centerpieces in rosy hues carried the heart-felt theme.

Patti Soskin, mother of the Bat Mitzvah girl, is a well-known Twin Cities food personality who owns Yum! Kitchen and Bakery. "I love working with Patti because she's so creative," Soile said. The result of their shared vision was the Kosher Valentine event at Temple of Aaron in St. Paul.

The wonderful thing about challah dough is that it is pliable. The loaf at each table was formed into a heart rather than a traditional braid. Patti found pink heart-shaped boxes, pre-set at each place, bountifully filled with green salad, fresh raspberries and strawberries, moistened with raspberry vinaigrette.

The entrée, Salmon Pot Pie, served in red bowls, was topped with heart-shaped puff pastry.

Lest we forget that Valentine's Day essential, chocolate, let's mention dessert: Chocolate cupcakes with pink icing, each bearing a heart-shaped lollipop.

Pink soft drinks were placed at every setting.

As guests left, they were overheard saying, "How fun was that?!"

TIP | Be creative with different types of containers.

Herbal greens with fresh fruit and Roquefort or goat cheese makes a refreshing salad.

Raspberry Vinaigrette

3 cups raspberries, fresh or frozen

1/2 cup balsamic vinegar

1/4 cup white wine vinegar

1 cup extra-virgin olive oil

1 teaspoon ginger

1/2 cup freshly-squeezed orange juice

Combine ingredients in blender and process until smooth.

Makes 3 cups.

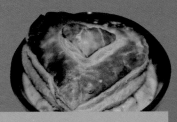

TIP | Brilliant bits of watermelon are "planted" with fresh flowers for bright centerpiece.

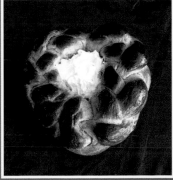

Heart-shaped challah loaves can be centered with honey butter. Cut out a circle large enough to hold a butter bowl.

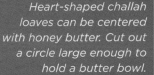

Salmon Pot Pies

2 cups cubed carrots	2-1/2 cups half and half
2 cups cubed potatoes	Salt and pepper to taste
1 cup cubed celery	1-1/2 cups cubed onion
2 cups salted water	3 cups cubed uncooked salmon
1/3 cup butter	2 cups frozen peas, thawed
1/3 cup all-purpose flour	1/2 cup chopped dill

Cut vegetables into small cubes that will cook quickly. Simmer carrots, potatoes and celery in salted water until tender.

In a saucepan over medium heat, melt the butter. Stir in the flour, mixing well. Add the half and half, salt and pepper. Continue stirring until the sauce thickens. Add onion and cook for about 5 minutes. Add cooked vegetables with any remaining liquid. Add the uncooked salmon cubes; cook about 15 minutes, stirring so mixture doesn't scorch. Stir in peas and dill; cook briefly. Spoon mixture into 8 warm serving bowls and top with rewarmed puff pastry hearts that have been previously baked.

Makes 8 servings.

Pink buttercream-iced chocolate cupcake adorned with heart-shaped marzipan lollipop.

Tie-Dye Whirl

Onion pies shared the colorful table with loaf-shaped Italian Tortas.

At a Tie-Dye party, tables and walls were festooned with fabrics dyed to suit the young celebrant's vision. Groovy!

Everything contributed to the theme, even the food. Plates in tie-dye patterns topped table coverings uniquely-colored in Hippie-era style. Tie-dyed hearts floated from the centerpieces, and the party cake was decorated in colorful whirls.

Onion pie, macaroni and cheese pie and Italian vegetable torta were served on platters arranged in tie-dye-like curvaceous patterns.

Focaccia bread bites surround olive caponata.

Onion Pie

Crust:

1-1/2 cups flour

6 tablespoons butter, cut in small pieces

1 tablespoon water

2 teaspoons vinegar

1 teaspoon salt

Filling:

2 tablespoon butter, cut in small pieces

4 large yellow onions, peeled and thinly sliced

1-1/2 tablespoons flour

1 cup heavy cream

2 eggs

1/4 teaspoon salt

Place flour in a bowl; add butter and rub flour and butter together by hand. Add water, vinegar and salt; knead until smooth. Cover and let dough rest for 15 minutes in refrigerator. Roll out dough and place in a greased quiche pan or large pie plate.

In a sauté pan, melt butter. Add onions and cook until soft and golden brown. Remove from heat. Spread the onion mixture over the crust. Combine flour, cream, eggs and salt. Pour over onions.If desired, add small cubes of butter on top. Bake in a 350-degree oven about 40 minutes. Slice into wedges and serve warm.

Makes 16 to 18 servings.

Sugar Cookies

1-1/4 cups sugar

2/3 cup butter

1 teaspoon pure vanilla

1 tablespoon orange juice

2 eggs

3 cups flour

2 teaspoons baking powder

1/2 teaspoon salt

In a large bowl, beat sugar, butter and vanilla until light and fluffy. Add orange juice and eggs; blend well. By hand, stir in flour, baking powder and salt until well blended. If the mixture seems dry, add another tablespoon of orange juice. If necessary refrigerate soft dough for easier handling.

Heat oven to 350 degrees. On a lightly-floured surface, roll out a third of the dough at a time to no more than 1/4-inch thickness. Keep remaining dough refrigerated. Cut with 2-1/2 to 3-inch cookie cutter. Place 2 inches apart on ungreased cookie sheets.

Bake for 9 to 12 minutes or until light golden brown. Cool 1 minute before removing from cookie sheets to finish cooling on racks or waxed paper. Repeat with remaining dough.

Makes 3 dozen cookies.

Chocolate cakes had tie-dyed frosting.

Sweet potato chips, baba ganoush, Kalamata olives and tuna sandwich loaf. See recipe on page 66.

For a hands-on experience in the art form, kids tie-dyed sugar cookies with tubes of colored frosting in battery-operated spinning machines.

TIP | As an extra treat, a rented machine produced spun sugar candy in a variety of hues.

Main courses were hot-off-the-grill shish kebabs, chicken or beef alternating with garden vegetables, or made-to-order omelets filled with local produce.

At the omelet station, a basket of fresh eggs was decorated with a goofy stuffed chicken.

Then guests picked up paper bags filled with plates, silverware, napkins and wine glasses — pulled into the party area in a Radio Flyer wagon. Inside a casually-styled tent, party-goers felt like they were shopping in farmers' market aisles, with displays of flowers, fruits, cheese, breads and local produce. Friends filled plates with an array of summer salads served from baskets. Tables were covered with burlap for a rustic, earthy effect.

farmers' market

A Twin Cities radio and print food journalist and cookbook author has been a devoted proponent of the local farmers' markets scene. She asked Soile to design a summer party at her Lake Minnetonka get-away home, and a Farmers' Market theme proved perfect. Crisp white tables, chairs and linen were set in a tree-shaded dining area overlooking the water. The idea can be adapted to any kind of summer celebration.

When guests arrived, they were offered miniature watermelon bowls filled with refreshing chilled watermelon soup.

Gramma Zelickson's Chocolate Cake

2 cups sugar

1 stick butter

3 ounces unsweetened chocolate

Hot water

3 eggs, separated

2 cups cake flour

1 teaspoon baking soda

1/2 teaspoon salt

1 cup buttermilk

1 teaspoon pure vanilla

Frosting:

2 cups sweetened condensed milk

1/8 teaspoon salt

2 cups semi-sweet chocolate chips

1/2 teaspoon pure vanilla

Heat oven to 350 degrees. Grease and flour an 8-inch round pan. Cream sugar and butter. Melt chocolate in a glass measuring cup; add enough hot water to measure 3/4 cup. Stir chocolate mixture into sugar mixture. Beat egg yolks; stir into chocolate mixture. Combine flour, soda and salt; add to mixture alternately with buttermilk. Beat egg whites until stiff peaks form. Fold into batter. Stir in vanilla. Pour into prepared pan. Bake about 40 to 50 minutes, or until a toothpick inserted in center comes out clean. Remove from pan and cool on a wire rack.

To make frosting:
Heat sweetened condensed milk with salt in the top of a double boiler. Mix well. Add the chocolate chips and cook over rapidly boiling water, stirring often, until thick, about 10 minutes. Remove from heat and cool. Sir in vanilla. Place cake layer on serving plate and cover top and sides with frosting.

Makes 1 cake.

An Evening in Africa

Africa inspired the décor for a
fundraising event benefiting the
Children's Hospital of St. Paul,
but the theme would be educational
for mitzvah kids who are enthusiastic
about saving the world and its animals.

The impressive cortile of the Landmark Center in St. Paul was transformed into "An Evening in Africa" with Deco Catering's fare and creative paper and straw animal figures fashioned by Richfield Flowers, a Twin Cities suburban florist.

The four-story space, dimly lighted, was draped with sheer fabric to resemble clouds through which a "full moon" shone on attendees. Tables for 300 guests were shaded by palm trees and the muted roars of African animals were heard in the background. Actual photos taken on safari were blown up to poster size to adorn walls, and music and dancers, tropical flowers and native masks created the effect of being transported to Africa.

A straw lion lorded over the buffet.

TIP | Tables dressed with straw skirting held antique wooden bowls and woks for serving platters.

47

Set against massive columns in the Landmark Center's cortile, the buffet table featured appetizing tidbits and salads served from woks to accommodate the large crowd. Serving spoons had animal-head handles and bamboo mats and palm leaves enhanced the effect.

Githeri | a Kenyan traditional dish of maize and beans boiled together.

Ugali | patties of maize, millet or sorghum flour (or a blend) cooked with water to a porridge-like consistency. Traditionally served with meat.

Irio | a mash combining potatoes with watercress and peas.

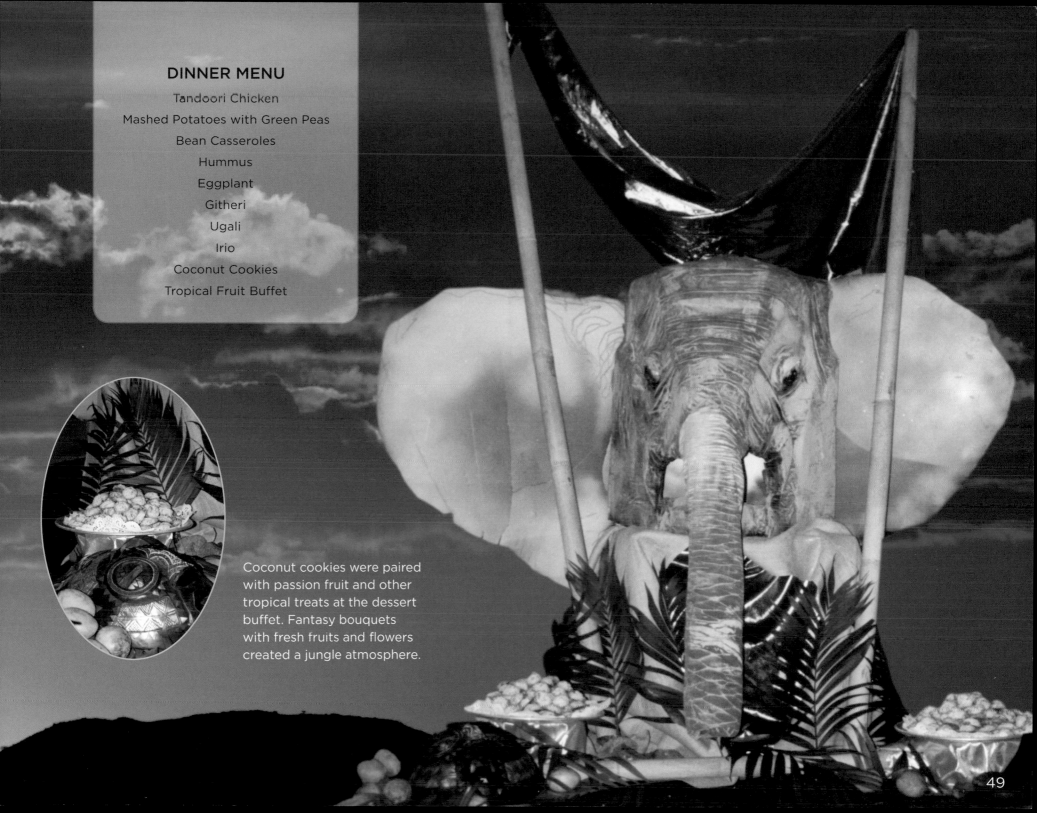

DINNER MENU
Tandoori Chicken
Mashed Potatoes with Green Peas
Bean Casseroles
Hummus
Eggplant
Githeri
Ugali
Irio
Coconut Cookies
Tropical Fruit Buffet

Coconut cookies were paired with passion fruit and other tropical treats at the dessert buffet. Fantasy bouquets with fresh fruits and flowers created a jungle atmosphere.

Feast Your Eyes

Especially after a long winter, Soile knows her clients are hungry for the visual feast and flavors she can create with salads and fruit displays.

At left, a Roman bacchanalia of garnet-colored grapes cascades amid platters of melon, peaches, apples and whatever else is in season. Buckets of tulips add multi-hues. Notice the lofty centerpiece carrying the eyes upward to more fruit and flowers.

Baked Brie encased in a sour cream dough crust and infused with raspberry or apricot jam is a favorite among Soile's clients. She serves it warm, surrounded by berries. If desired, bread slices or crackers can also accompany the molten cheese.

There are cheese platters, and then there's a Soile cheese platter, with picot-edged triangles and red pepper garnish, a few Bibb lettuce leaves tucked in for extra color.

Baked Brie with Sour Cream Dough

1 cup sour cream

2 sticks softened butter

2-1/2 cups flour

1 round Brie (about 2 pounds)

Good-quality raspberry jam

1 egg, beaten

Blend sour cream and soft butter. Add the flour, mixing well. Let dough rest for 30 minutes. Roll dough to medium thickness. Spread jam on top of Brie. Place dough over Brie and tuck underneath. With any scraps of dough, cut out decorations and place on top of dough-wrapped Brie. Brush with beaten egg. Bake at 350 degrees for 30 to 45 minutes, until crust is golden brown. Serve warm with berries and French bread or crackers.

The Sour Cream Dough can also be used for Salmon Wellington (recipe on page 21), quiches, Italian Tortas or savory pastries.

Makes 16 to 24 servings.

Cucumber-Tomato Salad

4 cups cucumbers

4 cups grape tomatoes

1/2 cup diced red onion

1/2 cup chopped cilantro

2 teaspoons salt

2 teaspoons black pepper

1/4 cup olive oil

2 teaspoons sugar

Mix all the vegetables. Combine salt, pepper, olive oil and sugar; pour over vegetables and toss well.

Makes 16 to 20 servings.

TIP | Onion "flowers" are a dramatic decoration for serving platters.

Salads are the color palette for your party. Fresh fruits, crisp greens, even exotic grains — preferably organic — create visual appeal.

Caponata Salad

2 eggplants, peeled and cut into cubes

1 cup olive oil

1 teaspoon salt

1 teaspoon black pepper

2 teaspoons olive oil

2 teaspoons crushed garlic

1 cup cubed onion

1/2 cup cubed red pepper

1/2 cup cubed yellow pepper

1 cup cubed celery

16 green olives

1/2 cup chopped Italian parsley

2 tablespoons Paul Prudhomme Vegetable Magic seasoning

3 tablespoons rice vinegar

Mix eggplant cubes with 1 cup olive. Season with salt and pepper. Roast in a 350-degree oven for 20 to 30 minutes, until lightly browned. In 2 teaspoons olive oil, sauté garlic and onion lightly. In a large bowl, combine eggplant, garlic, onion, red and yellow pepper, celery, olives and parsley. Season with Vegetable Magic and rice vinegar. Taste for additional salt and pepper. Allow to marinate for about an hour. Serve at room temperature.

Makes 12 to 14 servings.

Splashy Party

Clients who enjoy entertaining friends poolside — with a lakeside view — hosted a party with colorful, even organic fare. Sunny blue waters, tropical flowers and umbrellas, tiki torches and palm fronds — it could have been Hawaii or the Caribbean — but the setting was totally Minnesota.

Spoonfuls of Eggplant "Caviar" were among the passed appetizers.

Colorful linens and bright umbrellas were bathed with evening sunshine, a blessing of summer entertaining, which can extend to sunset and beyond. For the appetizer table centerpiece, some flowers were tucked inside the towering crystalline vase to hide stems, with more colorful blossoms rising upwards in stunning display. When entertaining outdoors, freshness is essential. Shown at left, organic veggies, propped with skewers, await being dipped into tangy sauces. Passed nibbles included Eggplant Caviar, Bruschettas and Mushroom Crostini (recipe on page 65). At a summer party, it's all about eye appeal and taste.

Casual food service at several stations inspired comfortable mingling. Guests gravitated to the potato bar where they found martini glasses heaped with mashed potatoes. They were invited to add sautéed vegetables and mushrooms, bits of barbecued beef and curried chicken. Cheese was available to sprinkle atop. At an adjoining grilling station they could choose from beef, chicken, lamb or vegetarian shish kebabs. Dessert was served at another station centered with a lofty chocolate fountain. Fresh fruit, sugar cookies and marshmallows were arranged for easy dipping.

Eggplant "Caviar"

1 large eggplant, oven-roasted for 30-45 minutes. Remove skin, chop eggplant and drain for several hours or overnight.

1 large onion, finely diced

2 tablespoons lemon juice

1 tablespoon vinegar

1 teaspoon salt

1 teaspoon ground black pepper

2 tablespoons tomato paste

1 tablespoon hot chili sauce

Combine ingredients, mixing well. Chill until ready to serve with little spoons, as shown in the photo at left.

Makes 6 cups.

TIP | Outdoor parties have their advantages. A dessert fountain flowing with liquid Belgian chocolate, served with cookies and fresh fruit for dipping at this soirée, would be a hazard to indoor carpeting. Chocolate fountains can be messy, but outside, no worries about drips.

What's an outdoor party without a lemonade stand?

A lofty arrangement of protea and other architectural flowers towers from a tall vase where stems are camouflaged by sunny yellow lemon halves. Lemonade made-to-order combined approximately 1/2 cup fresh squeezed lemonade sweetened with honey, spritzed to the top with sparkling mineral water. Ahh...refreshing!

Totally Pumpkin

Autumnal colors can inspire some dazzling dishes. Here, the culinary efforts are totally enhanced by creative serving ideas.

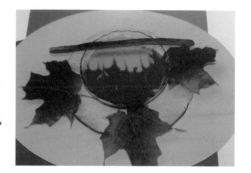

Imagine sitting at your place at the party and seeing the butternut squash and roasted pepper soup shown at right. Your eyes can't believe how beautiful it is. The two soups are ladled on opposite sides of the bowl, and then a steady hand traces orange hues into the gold. For a big party, imagine trekking to the woods to find enough colorful leaves to underscore the bowls. The solo breadstick balanced atop the bowl adds crunch to the experience.

Every party deserves a showstopper, a dish that is forever memorable.

Everyone associates pumpkins with fall, but not everyone envisions them as dishware. But they can be when the tops, seeds and inner strings are removed and a steaming portion of pumpkin or squash soup or a hearty stew fills the void. To keep contents hot, replace the "lid" with its convenient stem as a handle. Soile likes to serve the pumpkin fare with whole wheat bread textured with cranberries and walnuts.

Mashed Potatoes

Beef Stroganoff

TIP | Pumpkins can also be a carrier for hot foods. To make sure the contents, whatever they be, remain hot, pour boiling water into the pumpkin bowls. Drain before adding main entrees.

Roasted Parsnips

Roasted Parsnips

12 parsnips

1/4 cup maple syrup

1/4 cup olive oil

1 tablespoon Paul Prudhomme Vegetable Magic seasoning

1/2 stick butter, cubed

Peel and boil parsnips for 10 minutes. Halve parsnips lengthwise. On baking sheets lined with parchment paper spread olive oil. Place parsnip halves on the paper; drizzle with maple syrup and sprinkle with vegetable seasoning and butter cubes. Roast for 1/2 hour at 350 degrees.

Makes 12 servings.

AUTUMN MENU

Beef Stroganoff

Mashed Potatoes

Homemade Cranberry
Pear Chutney

Cucumber Salad

Roasted Red Beets

Roasted Carrots

Roasted Parsnips

Roasted Butternut Squash

Apple Pie with Ice Cream

Cranberry Pear Chutney

2 pounds cranberries

2 cups sugar

1 cup brown sugar

8 cups peeled and cubed pears

1 teaspoon nutmeg

1 teaspoon ginger

Place all ingredients in a heavy saucepan (this recipe does not use water). Boil slowly for 1 hour, until cranberries and pears are soft. Serve with stroganoff. Also excellent with Thanksgiving turkey or with plain Greek yogurt as a dessert or snack.

Makes 12 cups.

Olé, Olé, Let's Party Today!

On a buena blue-sky day, the setting wasn't Acapulco, though the decorations screamed Mexico. The party was in a Minnesota backyard where shrubbery provided the green and table linens added the red and green — those colors echoing the Mexican flag.

"It was a colorful atmosphere," recalls Soile, who created the food and decor that transported guests south of the border. Tables were shaded by umbrellas in rainbow hues. A mariachi band added tempo.

And then there was the food — all the familiar Mexican flavors but presented fiesta-style.

Everyone clustered around a dips bar loaded with black bean salad, guacamole, salsa and caterer-made tortilla chips to scoop it all onto plates. Margaritas with a kick or non-alcoholic kept guests happily hydrated on a hot afternoon.

A handle cactus with its needle-sharp spines is brave, indeed, but think of the visual impact of cactus paws amid a display of brilliant vegetables. Cactus paws can be purchased in Mexican markets, spines already removed.

If they weren't already satiated with appetizers, the main course filled everyone to the brim of their sombreros. They piled plates with chicken mole, roasted vegetables and hot rice studded with scrambled egg bits.

A colorfully-painted Central American cart holds black bean salad, salsa and guacamole, scooped by sturdy homemade tortilla chips.

Soile's Salsa (Pico de Gallo)

6 cups ripe tomatoes, finely chopped

2 cups finely chopped red onion

2 jalapeno peppers, seeded and finely chopped

1 cup chopped cilantro

2 teaspoons salt

4 teaspoons sugar

1 cup lime juice

Do all chopping by hand. Combine ingredients and taste to adjust seasonings, if necessary. Serve on Mexican buffet. Excellent with tacos and quesadillas.

Makes 8 cups.

Avocado Dressing

1 cup plain yogurt

1 clove garlic

1-1/2 to 2 tablespoons lime juice

1 cup heavy cream

2 to 3 ripe avocados, peeled and pitted

1 tablespoon minced chives

Salt and pepper to taste

Combine all ingredients in a blender, mixing until smooth. Taste to adjust lime juice, salt and pepper. Nice on romaine lettuce or other green salad.

Makes 3 cups.

TIP | Cut yellow squash lengthwise into quarters, coat with olive oil and vegetable seasoning; grill. To roast peppers, place on grill until skin is blackened, peel skin, remove seeds, cut into pieces and toss with olive oil, balsamic vinegar, salt and pepper to taste.

Gypsy Party

Corporate executives flew in on private jets from all over the country for a "mystery" party hosted by Sandy Grieve, then CEO of Ecolab in St. Paul, and his wife, Flo. The only clue on their invitations was "wear comfortable shoes."

Upon arrival at a wooded property on Sunfish Lake, south of St. Paul, they followed a straw-strewn path to a circular tent — not connected to electricity or running water. And suddenly, they were in a European-style Gypsy encampment, surrounded by staff wearing headscarves and flounced skirts. Should they need facilities, they were directed to Porta-Potties draped with old curtains (pictured left). Meanwhile, in underground pits lined with hot coals, marinated lamb legs wrapped in cabbage leaves and foil baked for six hours until ultra-tender. While waiting for the feast, guest snacked on herring, rustic breads and grilled chicken skewers passed around on dust pans while listening to gypsy stories spun by WCCO radio personality Bill Farmer.

Here comes the lamb after cooking for six hours underground.

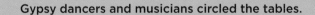

Multi-hued bandanas were table nappery and drinks were served in heavy ceramic mugs. With great pomp, the lamb was unearthed and carried on litters to be carved tableside and served with lingonberry sauce, cabbage and potatoes, the latter boiled in a black iron cauldron over a roaring fire. An old boat served as a buffet table featuring hot grilled salmon. Salads were piled in wooden barrels.

Gypsy dancers and musicians circled the tables.

And when all the potatoes were fished out of the cauldron, after-dinner coffee was boiled in that giant pot.

Smoked whole salmon, recipe on page 12.

Assorted herring and breads.

O Canada!

Every summer, the Canadian Consulate in Minneapolis hosts an event on the shores of Cedar Lake, and local business leaders look forward to their annual invitation.

To promote foodstuffs produced by our northern neighbor, the menu features Canadian bacon in various formats such as bacon-stuffed mushrooms, cheeses, fish, and a perennial favorite, sausages simmered in maple syrup. Smoked rainbow trout, lox salmon canapés and cubes of Canadian bacon skewered with cheese and grapes further the food theme.

Canada's national colors — red and white — are echoed by sugar cookies (recipe on page 43) shaped like maple leaves decked with red frosting, with two-tone sandwich cookies (recipe on page 25).

Every year, the centerpiece is a massive maple leaf ice carving. Two other icy salutes: shrimp with cocktail sauce served in a huge ice bowl, and elegant Canadian Eis Wine. No wonder people can't wait for next summer's party.

Taste of Canada: skewered cantaloupe, Canadian bacon and grapes.

Summer delight: cherry tomatoes, fresh mozzarella with basil.

Rooftop Nibbles au Natural

Sushi tuna on wonton skins.

TIP | Platters can be enhanced with edible decorations such as thinly-sliced acorn squash topped with a tomato rose.

Driving along the shore of Lake Superior, Soile spotted slabs of shale rock. "Aha, serving platters," she thought as she loaded her car with the gifts from nature.

Setting up the buffet for a Minneapolis rooftop appetizer party, she spread fresh moss garnered from a floral wholesaler, then heaved the rocks, oiled for luster, on top. "Very heavy," she admits, "but the wind couldn't blow them away."

Guests were offered unique martinis at the welcoming bar — ginger-flavored gin was popular. Then they were directed to the substantial hors d'oeuvres including homemade gravlax, shaved beef tenderloin atop horseradish-spread sourdough garnished with cucumber and cherry tomato, and asparagus spears rolled in ham and compressed bread. Sushi tuna quickly seared (both sides) then sliced ultra-thin while still slightly frozen, is perched on deep-fried wonton skins, with mayonnaise underneath and a kick of wasabi atop.

Out of sight but wafting tempting aromas over the rooftop were grills producing hot appetizers: lamb shish kebabs with ginger dressing, toasted Bruschetta and chicken sauté on sticks, passed to eager guests.

Peapods stuffed with herbed cream cheese.

Beef tenderloin open-face canapés, recipe on page 69.

Gravlax open-faced sandwiches, recipe on page 68. Served on Finnish Sourdough Rye Bread, recipe on page 77.

Roquefort cheese canapés with grapes.

Chicken sauté served with apricot glaze.

TIP | Keep your eyes open when you are on a nature drive. You can find beautiful platters for your tables.

63

Amazing Appetizers

Sun-dried tomatoes blended with cream cheese, olive oil, salt and pepper can be piped on cucumber rounds, pumpernickel, toast or crackers.

Deviled eggs garnished with red-pepper and parsley.

If budget allows, a fabulous ice carving showcased on its own table can be both centerpiece and chilled server when piled with shrimp, cocktail sauce and lots of lemons. Be prepared to replenish frequently.

Mushroom Crostini

16 thin slices of rough-textured artisan bread (use a slender loaf), such as ciabatta or sourdough

6 tablespoons olive oil, divided

Salt

3 garlic cloves divided

1 pound small portobello mushrooms, thinly sliced

1/4 teaspoon salt

1 tablespoon balsamic vinegar

1/4 cup flat-leafed parsley, finely chopped

8 ounces soft goat cheese

Finely chopped fresh chives

Grated zest of 1 orange

Heat the oven to 400 degrees. On a non-stick baking pan, place bread slices. Combine 3 tablespoons olive oil and 1 crushed garlic clove; brush bread with oil and sprinkle with salt. Bake for 6 minutes until lightly browned around edges and crisped.

For the topping, heat remaining 3 tablespoons oil in a sauté pan over medium-high heat. Sauté 2 chopped garlic cloves for 1 minute. Add the mushrooms and 1/4 teaspoon salt, stirring to coat with the garlic mixture. Sauté for 4 minutes, or until the mushroom soften. Add vinegar and parsley, tossing to mix. Remove from the heat.

Into soft goat cheese, stir in chopped chives to taste. Add salt and pepper if desired. Spread about 1 tablespoon goat cheese mixture on the each bread slice. Spoon on some mushroom mixture. Garnish with grated orange zest.

Makes 16 servings.

For another version of crostini, mix goat cheese with fresh chopped basil, olive oil, salt and pepper. Cover warm toasted slices of garlic bread (directions in recipe above for Mushroom Crostini) with goat cheese mixture, and garnish with halved cherry tomatoes. Serve immediately.

A flower-bedecked serpentine table offers an appetizer array displayed on many levels to please both eye and palate. Burlap was draped on the buffet for this party staged in Soile's back yard.

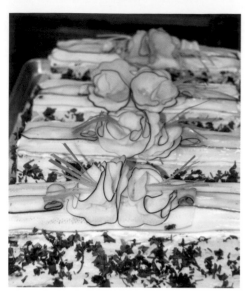

Sandwich loaf adorned with summer squash ribbons.

Salmon Mousse

8 ounces cream cheese

1 clove of garlic, chopped

1/2 cup fresh dill, chopped

Salt and pepper to taste

8 ounces smoked salmon

Whip cream cheese in mixer. Add remaining ingredients and whip until smooth. Fills one layer of a sandwich loaf.

Sandwich Loaf

2 loaves of Pullman bread, white and pumpernickel

Salmon mousse

Egg salad

Tuna salad

24 ounces softened cream cheese flavored with fresh garlic, salt, pepper and fresh dill

Chopped parsley

Summer squash cut into thin ribbons

Equal parts of apricot jelly and water, heated to form a glaze

Have the bakery slice Pullman loaves horizontally. On a sheet of parchment paper, place a slice of pumpernickel bread and spread generously with salmon mousse. Add a layer of white bread and top with egg salad. Repeat with pumpernickel and tuna salad. Top with white bread slice. For a taller sandwich loaf, repeat layers. Wrap tightly with parchment paper and allow to rest for 2 hours in refrigerator.

Before frosting, unwrap loaf and with a serrated bread knife trim any crust and uneven edges. Place loaf on a serving platter. Frost with seasoned cream cheese. Press chopped parsley on top and sides. Using slices of summer squash, decorate the top of the loaf to resemble ribbons and bows. To keep squash moist and shiny, brush with apricot glaze. Chill until sliced and served.

Makes 10 to 12 servings.

Double-sized seafood sandwich loaf decorated with shrimp.

Tuna Salad

12 ounce of Albacore tuna

1/2 cup finely-chopped celery

1 cup finely-chopped yellow onion

1/2 cup chopped fresh dill

1 tablespoon pepper

1 cup of real mayonnaise

Juice of 1/2 lime

Salt to taste

Mix ingredients together and chill. Fills one layer of a sandwich loaf.

Egg Salad

6 hard-cooked eggs, peeled and chopped

1/2 to 3/4 cup real mayonnaise

1/2 cup chopped parsley

1/2 cup chopped red pepper

Salt and pepper to taste

Mix ingredients together and chill. Fills one layer of a sandwich loaf.

Pea and Salmon Samosas

1 large potato, boiled and roughly mashed

2 tablespoons vegetable oil

1 small onion, finely chopped

1 clove garlic, finely chopped

1 tablespoon grated fresh ginger

Salt and pepper to taste

1 teaspoon ground cumin

1 cup fresh or frozen peas

1/2 cup chopped cilantro

1-1/2 cups chopped fresh salmon

Square spring roll wrappers

1 egg white, lightly beaten

3 cups vegetable oil

Place potato in a bowl. In 2 tablespoons oil in a sauté pan, lightly cook onion, garlic and ginger. Add to potato. Season with salt, pepper and cumin. Stir peas, cilantro and salmon into potato mixture. Place about 1 tablespoon potato mixture on the center of a spring roll wrapper. Brush edges of dough with beaten egg white. Fold dough in half into a triangle and press edges together to seal well. Continue until all of dough and filling are used. In vegetable oil heated to 375 degrees, fry samosas until golden brown. Drain on paper towels. Serve with strawberry-rhubarb chutney or mango chutney.

Makes 40 samosas.

Herring Open-Faced Sandwiches

2 cups pickled herring, finely chopped

1 cup sour cream

1 Granny Smith apple, peeled, cored and finely chopped

1/2 cup finely chopped yellow onion

1 teaspoon white pepper

Salt to taste

2 tablespoon chopped dill

2 tablespoons chopped fresh chives

Cocktail-sized pumpernickel bread

Soft butter

Butter lettuce

Sprigs of fresh dill

Fresh chives

Small wedges of lemon

Hand-mix the herring, sour cream, apple and onion. Add white pepper. Add salt to taste, chopped dill and chives. Butter slices of pumpernickel bread as needed. Place a piece of butter lettuce on a slice of bread. Spoon on some of the herring mixture. Spreading slightly. Garnish with a sprig of fresh dill, a piece of fresh chive and a small wedge of lemon.

Makes 30 servings.

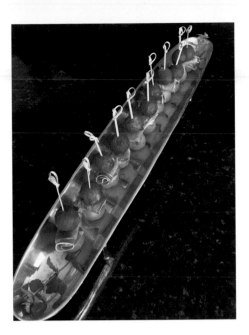

Prosciutto Melon Balls

1 large ripe cantaloupe, halved and seeded

1/2 ripe watermelon, seeded

4 to 6 slices lean prosciutto, thinly sliced

24 cocktail picks

Using the large end of a melon-baller, scoop each melon into 24 balls. Cut each slice of the Italian ham lengthwise into thirds, then crosswise in half. Chill the melon and ham.

To assemble, fold prosciutto and place between canalope and watermelon balls, using a cocktail pick to secure in place. Serve quickly before the melon juice discolors and softens the prosciutto.

Makes 24 servings.

Beef Tenderloin Open-Face Canapés

1 beef tenderloin, about 3 pounds, seasoned with olive oil, freshly-ground pepper and finely-minced garlic
(for extra kick, use some cayenne pepper)

1 loaf Finnish Sourdough Rye Bread (recipe on page 77)

Softened butter

Whole grain mustard

Thinly-sliced cucumbers

Cherry tomatoes, halved

Parsley leaves

Season beef tenderloin. Cover with plastic wrap and allow to marinate in the refrigerator overnight. Unwrap, sprinkle with salt, and grill to 120 degrees (medium rare). Let it rest at least two hours.

To make canapés: Trim ends of tenderloin to make the meat of uniform thickness. Slice tenderloin very thin, about 1/4 inch. Use a 2-inch cookie cutter to cut rounds from medium-thin slices of sourdough bread. Spread bread rounds with softened butter and mustard (or use creamy horseradish for more tang). Place a slice of tenderloin on each round, pushing it to make it the same size as the bread. Decorate with fanned cucumbers, a cherry tomato half and a leaf of parsley. Serve as soon as possible.

Makes 50 to 60 servings.

Soile's home-cured gravlax are brightened with lemon wedges and dill served on sourdough bread.

Lox Salmon — Gravlax

2 fresh wild salmon fillets, about 1-1/2 pounds each

1/3 cup Kosher salt, divided

1 cup fresh dill weed

1 tablespoon sugar

1 tablespoon pickling spice

1 tablespoon whole peppercorns

1/4 cup good quality vodka

Whole dill sprigs

Place salmon fillets, flesh side up, on a baking sheet lined with parchment paper. Sprinkle both fillets with about half of the salt. Cover with fresh dill weed. Sprinkle with sugar, pickling spice and peppercorns, pressing into fish. Turn fillets over. Sprinkle with remaining salt. Drizzle with vodka. Cover generously with whole stalks of fresh dill. Cover with parchment paper, and place another baking sheet on top with the bottom of the sheet facing down. Place a brick wrapped in foil on top of the upper pan. Place in the refrigerator for one to two days to marinate. Slice gravlax thinly to serve.

Makes 30 to 40 servings.

TIP | Half of an unpeeled honeydew or cantaloupe can support fruit skewers for an edible centerpiece.

Lobster Quesadillas

1 6-inch tortilla

1 slice Monterey Jack cheese

1/4 cup chopped lobster meat

1 tablespoon butter, melted

1 teaspoon salsa

1 teaspoon chipotle sour cream

Place tortilla on a cutting board and place cheese slice in the middle. Place lobster on top of cheese. Melt butter in a sauté pan. Fold tortilla in half and place in heated pan. Cook until golden brown. Flip and cook until the other side is browned. Place tortilla on cutting board and cut into three triangles. Garnish each triangle with Pepper Salsa and Chipotle Sour Cream.

Makes 1 serving.

New red potatoes, briefly boiled, then scooped, are seasoned and roasted, filled with dill dressing (page 85) and capers before serving hot.

Pepper Salsa

1/2 cup finely-diced red bell pepper

1/2 cup finely-diced yellow bell pepper

3/4 cup finely-diced green pepper

2 tablespoons minced jalapeno pepper with seeds

2 teaspoons chipotle pesto

1/2 cup diced green onion

1 tablespoon fresh lime juice

1/2 teaspoon salt

3 tablespoon minced cilantro

Combine all ingredients and place in a covered container. Refrigerate until ready to use. Use to garnish Lobster Quesadillas.

Makes 2 cups.

Chipotle Sour Cream

1 cup sour cream

2 tablespoons chipotle pesto

1/2 teaspoon salt

1-1/2 teaspoons fresh lime juice

Combine all ingredients and place in a covered container. Refrigerate until ready to use. Use to garnish Lobster Quesadillas.

Makes 1 cup.

Indulging in Delectable Desserts!

Entertaining can be elegantly simple — an afternoon gathering offering memorable desserts, champagne and coffee. Whatever the celebration, who can resist cakes and other goodies galore?

Soile invites guests to sample from a platter of chocolate-dipped strawberries and fresh blueberry-vanilla cream tarts. Cakes, intensely-flavored and lavishly decorated, might include lemon layer cake filled with fresh lemon mousse, a chocolate raspberry torte, blueberry coffee cake or apple tart.

When Alton Brown from the Food Network asked Soile to do a dessert buffet, she made her classic berry-studded Helsinki Torte, sandbakkels and a towering Kransekake.

Individual dense cakes decorated with rollled marzipan to look like gift boxes.

Norwegian Sandbakkels filled with chocolate mousse.

Lemon Cake filled with lemon mousse.

Chocolate layer cake with fresh raspberries.

Blueberry Coffee Cake

1-1/2 cups flour	3 eggs
1-1/4 cups sugar	1 teaspoon vanilla
1-1/2 teaspoons baking powder	1-1/2 cups of fresh blueberries (or lingonberries)
2 sticks cold butter, cut into cubes	1/3 cup apricot jelly

Mix flour, sugar and baking powder in a mixer, using the paddle blade. Add butter cubes, 1/2 stick at a time, while mixer is on low speed, until a fluffy paste forms. Crack eggs one at a time in a separate bowl. Slowly add 1 egg at a time, with mixer at low speed. Add vanilla. Grease and flour a 9-inch round cake pan, preferably one with a removable bottom. Place batter in pan. Sprinkle blueberries on top of batter. Bake in a 350-degree oven for 45 minutes, or until a toothpick comes out clean. If not done, lower temperature and bake longer. Remove cake from oven and cool. Remove from pan. If not serving immediately, wrap and freeze. If using right away, briefly simmer apricot jelly with a small amount of water, stirring until smooth; brush warm glaze over cake.

Makes 1 cake.

Apple Tart

Crust:

1 cup flour

1/3 cup powdered sugar

1 stick cold butter, cut into small pieces

Filling:

8 ounces cream cheese, softened

1/4 cup sugar

1 large egg

1/2 teaspoon pure vanilla

Topping:

4 Granny Smith apples, peeled and cut into 1/4-inch slices

1/3 cup granulated sugar

1/2 teaspoon ground cinnamon

Preheat oven to 450 degrees and place rack in the center of the oven. Grease and flour a 9-inch springform pan (or use Baker's Joy to prepare the pan).

To make the crust: In the bowl of a food processor place the flour and sugar. Pulse to blend together. Add butter and pulse until dough begins to come together. Pat the dough onto the bottom and one inch up the sides of the pan. Cover with plastic wrap and place in the refrigerator while making the filling.

To make the filling: In a food processor process the cream cheese until smooth. Add the sugar and mix well. Blend in the egg and vanilla. Process until smooth. Remove the crust from the refrigerator and pour in the filling. Return to the refrigerator while the topping is prepared.

For the topping: Arrange the apple slices over the cream cheese filling. Combine the sugar and cinnamon; sprinkle over apples.

Bake for 10 minutes. Reduce the heat to 350 degrees and bake for 25 to 30 minutes until golden brown and apples are soft when pierced with a fork. Filling should be almost set. Spread with apricot glaze (see the Blueberry Coffee Cake at left for instructions). Serve at room temperature.

Makes 1 tart.

Lingonberry Torte

3 sticks butter, softened

1-1/2 cups granulated sugar

2 eggs

2 teaspoons vanilla

1 cup Cream of Wheat cereal

2 cups flour

2-1/2 teaspoons baking powder

1 cup frozen lingonberries, thawed and drained

2 cups heavy cream, whipped with 1 cup powered sugar

Preheat the oven to 350 degrees. Butter and lightly flour two 8-inch round cake or tart pans or one 12-inch tart pan.

In a large mixer bowl, cream together butter and sugar until light and fluffy. Beat in the eggs one at a time. Beat in the vanilla. Blend the Cream of Wheat, flour and baking powder. Mix the dry ingredients into the butter-sugar mixture, beating well. Spread the dough into the prepared pans. Sprinkle with the lingonberries. Bake for about 20 minutes or until golden brown. Let cool in pans for 5 minutes before turning out onto plates. Allow to cool thoroughly. Dust with powdered sugar or garnish with sweetened whipped cream and more lingonberries. Makes two 8-inch cakes or one 12-inch cake. They freeze beautifully. You could substitute blueberries or other firm fruit for the lingonberries.

Makes two 8-inch round cakes or one 12-inch tart pan.

Summertime treats: jumbo stem-on strawberries dipped in white and dark chocolate, circled by Norwegian blueberry sandbakkels.

Date-Buckwheat Coffee Cake

2-1/2 cups dates	2 eggs
1-1/2 cups water	2 teaspoons vanilla
1 cup sugar	1 teaspoon soda
2 sticks soft butter (reserve 1 tablespoon for greasing cake pan)	1 teaspoon baking powder
	2 cups buckwheat flour

Combine dates, water and sugar in a saucepan and boil until dates are soft. Cool. Place mixture in a blender or food processor. Processing until smooth. Place date mixture into an electric mixing bowl. Add butter to date mixture; blend. Add eggs and vanilla; blend again. Combine soda, baking powder and buckwheat flour. Sift into mixer. Combine well. With the reserved tablespoon of butter, grease a Bundt pan. Place batter in pan. Bake at 350 degrees for 1 hour. After removing from oven, turn pan upside down to cool. Place on serving plate. Keeps well.

Makes 1 cake.

Soile's Spectacular Chocolate Cake

Cake:

12 ounces semi-sweet chocolate chips

1 tablespoon pure vanilla

1 tablespoon rum or Grand Marnier

1/4 cup espresso coffee

5 large eggs

1/2 cup granulated sugar

Ganache:

2 cups semi-sweet chocolate chips

1 cup heavy cream

1 teaspoon butter

Centering the cake is a chocolate rose enhanced with gold dust.

Preheat the oven to 325 degrees. Coat a 10-inch springform pan with butter and wrap the outside of the pan with a double thickness of aluminum foil to prevent water from seeping in.

Place the chocolate chips, vanilla, rum and coffee in the top of a double boiler over 1 inch of simmering (not boiling) water. Whisk until the chocolate is smooth and no lumps remain. Transfer the chocolate mixture to a large bowl and let it cool.

In a medium mixing bowl, combine the eggs and sugar. With electric mixer, beat until pale in color, stopping two or three times to scrape down the sides of the bowl. Add 1/4 of the cooled chocolate mixture and beat until incorporated. Pour this mixture into the remaining chocolate; stir until combined. Pour the mixture into the prepared cake pan.

Place prepared cake pan into a roasting pan and add enough boiling water to come halfway up the outside of the cake pan. Bake for 30 minutes until small cracks appear on the surface. Remove the roasting pan from the oven and lift cake pan to cool on a wire rack. Leave cake in pan while it cools.

To make ganache: In the top of a double boiler over simmering water, melt chocolate chips. Add heavy cream and butter, stirring until smooth.

Unmold the cake and place on a dessert plate. Pour chocolate ganache over the cake, spreading to smooth. Use melted white chocolate in a pastry bag to decorate, as shown. Chill until served.

Makes 12 to 14 servings.

Carrot-Zucchini Loaves

4 cups sugar

8 eggs

3 cups oil

4 cups flour

1 tablespoon baking powder

1 tablespoon soda

1 tablespoon salt

2 tablespoons cinnamon

2 cups shredded carrots

2 cups shredded zucchini

2 cups chopped walnuts

2 cans (20 ounces each) pineapple tidbits, drained

In a large mixing bowl with paddle attachment, cream sugar and eggs. Slowly add oil until mixture is fluffy. Combine dry ingredients in a bowl, then add them to the batter, mixing well. Shred carrots and zucchini. Place drained pineapple tidbits in a food processor and pulse briefly so pineapple remains coarse. Place pineapple in a strainer and press to drain well. Add the carrots, zucchini, walnuts and pineapple to the flour mixture.

Spray four loaf pans. Cut strips of parchment paper and use them to line pans. Divide batter among the four pans. Bake in a 350-degree oven for about 45 minutes or until a toothpick comes out clean.

Makes 4 loaves.

Norsk Holiday Buffet

Soile may be a Finn, but she frequently caters parties for all ethnic Scandinavians, such as this Norwegian holiday buffet, known as a Julebord.

It wouldn't be a Norsk Christmas celebration without air-dried lamb leg, cut in paper-thin slices, or without Norwegian ribs imbued with a flavorful marinade, then oven-roasted until the fat and skin are crispy. Piquant creamy horseradish sauce is the complement. So are potatoes, so basic to all Scandinavians meals. Herring and gravlax are essential, as the menu indicates.

Decor depends heavily on reds and greens, especially fresh boughs which add their own scent to the event. Crimson tulips carry the color theme and also hint at springtime to come. Lots and lots of candles add glow to the holiday party, staged on one of the darkest days of the year.

Lingonberry sauce is a "must" for any Nordic buffet. Simply combine fresh or thawed frozen lingonberries with enough sugar to temper the tanginess.

Herbed cream cheese fashioned into snowmen, capped with red pepper "hats," are ready to spread on flat bread.

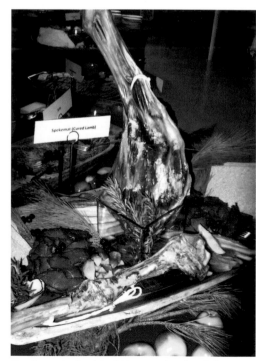

Spekemat air-dried Norwegian lamb leg.

Scrambled Eggs (served cold)

TIP | Horseradish sauce, Finnish-style, combines whipped cream, sugar, vinegar and salt and pepper to taste. Give it zing with freshly-grated horseradish.

Norwegian Pork Ribs

Slab of pork ribs, with fat and skin attached

Rub:

2 teaspoons freshly-ground black pepper

1 teaspoon dried sage

1 teaspoon ground allspice

1 teaspoon ground cloves

1/2 cup brown sugar

Salt

1 to 1-1/2 cups apple juice

Combine the pepper, sage, allspice, cloves and brown sugar. Rub on all sides of the ribs. Let marinate, refrigerated, for several hours or overnight. Just before baking, sprinkle generously with salt. Place ribs in a 400-degree oven and roast, skin-side up, until the skin becomes crispy. Add apple juice to the pan and cover tightly with foil. Lower temperature to 300 degrees and bake until the meat is done. Slice between every other rib bone and serve warm on a platter, skin-side up. Make a gravy with the pan juices and serve with the ribs.

Serves 6 to 8.

Krumkaka Norwegian Cookies

3 eggs

1 stick butter, melted

3/4 cup flour

1/2 cup sugar

1/2 teaspoon freshly-ground cardamom, or more to taste

Combine well eggs, melted butter, flour, sugar and cardamon in a bowl. Spray a hot krumkaker pan with cooking spray; wipe off excess. Place about 1 tablespoon (or less) of batter on the hot iron and close handles. Brown about 1 minute. Remove from iron and roll cookie on a cone or dowel while it is still very warm. Makes 2 to 3 dozen cone cookies. Recipe contributed by Soile's friend Sharon Severson, who got it while traveling in Norway.

Makes 2 to 3 dozen.

Julebord Buffet Meny

Gravlaks • Herring in wine sauce • Deviled eggs
Sylte • Spekemat (cured leg of lamb)

Herb Roasted Wild Alaskan Salmon served with Dill Sauce
Marinated Cucumber salad • "Ribbe" (pork ribs)
Medisterpølse • Gravy
Surkál (Red Norwegian sauerkraut)
Kálrabistappe (rutabaga) • Ertestuing (peas)
Baby Red Potatoes with fresh dill • Herb Mashed Potatoes
Lingonberries • Flatbread • Lefse • Butter

Dessert Served Tableside (Family Style)
Riskrem (rice cream with berry sauce)
Krumkaker

Traditional Norwegian Cake Parade
and kaffebord
Karamellpudding • Kransekake
Flourless Chocolate Pastries • Marsipankake • Almond Bites

Coffee • Tea • Non-alcoholic Beer
Sparkling Lingonberry Juice

Presented by Deco Catering
Soile Anderson

FINNISH CHRISTMAS

Soile's childhood memories of Christmas Eve on the family farm in Finland are burnished by time and polished by tradition. "When I was a little girl, it was such an exciting day, and the house smelled so wonderful from cooking aromas and the pine tree that was brought in that day for decorating. We would, before dinner, go to the barn to give the animals an extra treat of food. Then, as everyone gathered, cups of Glöki (hot spiced wine flavored with orange peel, raisins and cinnamon sticks) were poured." Children sipped hot apple cider.

Dinner was served family-style, but eaten in stages. First, pickled herring and gravlax. Then a slice of headcheese. Then the meats, vegetables, beet salad and rutabaga casserole. After dinner as gifts were opened, coffee and prune tarts, ginger cookies and rice pudding with prune compote were served. These recipes give you a taste of Finnish Christmas, which Soile has always prepared for her family and for catered Suomi holiday feasts.

Sourdough Fruit Bread

Finnish Sourdough Rye Bread dough on the fifth day (see page 77)

Your choice of dried fruits such as figs, pears, glazed orange peels, glazed lemon peels, plums and raisins, totaling 8 cups

Dark rum to moisten the fruits

1/2 cup freshly grated lemon peel

1 cup brewed black coffee

2 teaspoons powdered cloves

Nuts of choice, such as pine nuts, walnuts or pecans

Dice dried fruit and soak covered for 5 days in dark rum. On the fifth day of the bread-making process, add fruit, lemon peel, coffee and powdered cloves to the starter. Continue following instructions for adding yeast, salt and enough flour to form a firm dough. Cover bowl and allow the dough to double in size. Divide dough into 6 portions and shape into round loaves. Raise until the surface forms fine cracks. Before baking, brush loaves with additional black coffee and decorate with choice of nuts. Bake at 350 degrees for 1 hour and 15 minutes. Excellent toasted with butter.

Makes 6 large loaves.

Finnish Sourdough Rye Bread

Starter

12 cups water, slightly warmed

3 tablespoons dry yeast

6 cups stone-ground rye flour

Second Day

3 cups stone-ground rye flour

Third Day

3 cups stone-ground rye flour

Fourth Day

3 cups stone-ground rye flour

Fifth Day

1 tablespoons dry yeast

4 tablespoons salt

About 12 cups additional stone-ground rye flour to firm the dough

Starter: In a large container combine warm (not hot) water, 3 tablespoons yeast and 6 cups rye flour. Cover the container and allow the starter to stand at room temperature for a day. Check to make sure bubbles are forming.

On the second day: Add 3 cups of rye flour, recover the container and allow to stand another day at room temperature while starter continues to bubble.

On the third day: Add 3 cups of rye flour, recover the container and allow to stand another day at room temperature while starter continues to bubble.

On the fourth day: Add 3 cups of rye flour, recover the container and allow to stand another day at room temperature while starter continues to bubble.

On the fifth day: Put the starter into a large mixing bowl and add another 1 tablespoon of yeast and the salt. Mix in enough rye flour to make a firm dough. Cover bowl and allow the dough to double in size. Divide dough into 6 portions and shape into round loaves. Raise until the surface forms fine cracks. Bake loaves at 350 degrees for 1 hour and 15 minutes. Use to make open-face sandwiches with gravlax and other toppings.

For a more sour flavor, the starter can be kept at room temperature for an additional day or two, adding a little more flour each day, making sure the mixture continues to bubble.

Makes 6 large loaves.

TYPICAL FINNISH CHRISTMAS MENU

Two Different Kinds of Herring

Gravlax with Dilled Potatoes

Finnish Sourdough Rye Bread and Butter

Karelian Pies with Egg Butter

Head Cheese with Lingonberries

Rossolle — Red Beet Herring Salad

Rutabaga Casserole

Carrot Casserole

Liver Casserole

Lutefisk

Roasted Bone-in Ham

Sautéed Red Cabbage with Apples

Rice Pudding

Prune Tarts

Ginger Cookies

Rutabaga Casserole

2 rutabagas, peeled and cubed, cooked in salted water until soft

4 tablespoons butter

1 tablespoon flour

1/2 cup heavy cream

1/2 cup dark corn syrup or maple syrup

2 eggs

Salt and white pepper

Bread crumbs

Bits of butter

Mash cooked and drained rutabagas. Add butter, flour, cream, syrup and eggs, mixing well. Add salt and white pepper to taste. Butter an ovenproof casserole dish. Put rutabaga mixture into dish. Top with bread crumbs and dot with butter. Bake at 350 degrees for 45 minutes to an hour, until golden brown. Makes a nice side dish with baked ham.

Makes 12 or more servings.

Scandinavian Cole Slaw

2 heads fresh cabbage, remove core, and slice leaves very thin

2 onions, sliced very thin

2 cups chopped fresh dill

2 to 3 cups freshly-squeezed lemon juice

2 cups sugar

Salt and pepper to taste

Combine sliced cabbage and onion with remaining ingredients; stir well. Marinate, chilled, for 2 hours before serving.

Makes 12 or more servings.

Captain's Herring

4 good-sized pickled herring, cut into fillets, then cut again into bite-sized pieces

2 whole carrots, pared and cut crosswise into "coins"

2 small red onions, cut into rings

6 garlic cloves

2 bay leaves

1 tablespoon chopped fresh dill

2 cups water

2 cups vinegar

1 cup sugar

6 whole cloves

6 whole allspice

1 teaspoon mustard seed

In a large wide-mouth glass jar, layer herring, carrots, red onion rings, garlic cloves and bay leaves, sprinkling fresh dill between layers. In a saucepan, combine water, vinegar, sugar, whole cloves, allspice and mustard seed. Boil together until sugar dissolves and spices release their flavors. Cool liquid. Pour over herring and vegetables. Cover the jar. Marinate overnight in the refrigerator. Will keep a week or more.

Makes 12 or more servings.

Mustard Herring

4 good-sized pickled herring, cut into fillets, then cut again into bite-sized pieces

1 tablespoon sugar

3 tablespoons mild prepared mustard

2 tablespoons cooking oil

1 cup sour cream

2 tablespoons chopped dill

1 cup red onion rings

Lemon wedges

Pickled herring can be purchased at Scandinavian specialty stores, such as Ingebretsen's in Minneapolis, or IKEA. Arrange herring pieces on a platter. To make the sauce, combine sugar, mustard, oil, sour cream and dill, mixing well. Spoon sauce over herring. Decorate platter with red onion rings, lemon wedges and additional fresh dill sprigs.

Makes 12 or more servings.

Rossolle — Red Beet Herring Salad

6 cups red beets, boiled, peeled and cubed (reserve cooking liquid)

3 cups boiled potatoes, peeled and cubed

1 medium onion, chopped

2 cups carrots, pared, boiled and cubed

1 cup Granny Smith apple, peeled and cubed

1 cup dill pickles, cubed

2 cups of chopped pickled herring

Salt and pepper to taste

1 cup of white vinegar or more to taste

1/2 cup sugar

Salad dressing:

2 cups heavy cream, whipped

3 tablespoons powdered sugar

1 tablespoon vinegar

2 tablespoons (or more) red beet cooking juice

Mix evenly-diced beets, potatoes, onion, carrots, apple, dill pickles and herring in a large bowl. Season with salt and pepper to taste. Stir together vinegar and sugar; pour over cubed ingredients. Cover. Refrigerate for at least a day for flavors to blend.

Combine whipped cream, powdered sugar, vinegar and enough beet liquid to color it pink. Pipe pink whipped cream on top of salad. Sprinkle with capers, if desired. Serve as a first course on a holiday table.

Makes 12 cups.

Weddings

Gorgeous settings and glamorous touches on this and following pages showcase wonderful weddings, casual or elegant.

Villa Bellezza Winery and Vineyards in Pepin, Wisconsin (far left) exudes Italian charm and is among Soile's favorite venues. Set on a bluff overlooking Lake Pepin, it's an elegant destination, made even more so when the Villa's staff lavishly sets tables with votive candles, flowers, fresh rosemary and fragrant herbs in abundance (top left). When it was time to have wedding cake, each table was centered with a Norwegian Kransekake (bottom left) festooned with ribbons. Guests just had to reach for a ring of almond-flavored cake.

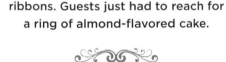

Little touches make a wedding memorable, as shown at Cindie Sinclair's rural Stillwater farm venue (right). Traditional Finnish tiered wedding cake (recipe on page 93), filled with chocolate mousse (recipe on page 37) was decorated with fresh roses. An antique cart becomes a place to display name cards for arriving guests. Tree branches — the epitome of free decorations — are wired to the backs of chairs to give the feel of dining in a bower. Instead of prosaic cloths, glistening runners draped on tables are a special touch that make friends and family say, "Aaahh."

Additional wedding inspirations can be seen at www.decocatering.com.

Romantic Country Wedding Venue

Stillwater is the most romantic of historical Minnesota villages, and just outside of town is a farm-turned-events-center where fairy-tale weddings can come true.

"I have done summer weddings for 20 years at Cindie Sinclair's Camrose Hill," where a permanent tent, a flower-bedecked wedding chapel for marriages of any denomination and all the accoutrement are already in place. All that's needed is the menu, ready to savor. "It has such a wonderful atmosphere, one of my very favorite places to cater," says Soile. "Cindie has such a creative mind, decorating chandeliers with flowers and candles, adding sparkling lights to an overhead bower of vines." Cherubs, love birds, flowers everywhere — the setting exudes romance.

"I match the food to the earthy surroundings, serving organic salads in antique bowls, and using kale and other natural elements to decorate the buffet."

The bride and groom are enthroned on baronial antique chairs during the wedding feast.

Wild Rice Cranberry Salad

3 pounds wild rice, cooked and cooled (follow package directions)

3 cups diced carrots (cook carrots until semi-tender before dicing)

3 cups diced zucchini

8 red peppers, seeded and diced

2 onions, diced

1-1/2 cups diced celery

1/2 cup chopped fresh basil

3 cups dried cranberrles

Dressing:

2 cups olive oil

1/2 cup rice vinegar

1 tablespoon black pepper

2 tablespoons finely-chopped garlic

Salt and pepper to taste

Combine wild rice with carrots, zucchini, red pepper, onion, celery, basil and cranberries in a large mixing bowl. Combine dressing ingredients and pour over wild rice mixture. Mix well. Chill to blend flavors.

If desired, 3 cups chopped smoked rainbow trout or smoked whitefish can be added to the salad. Soile smokes the fish on a Weber grill.

Makes 40 to 50 servings.

TIP | Ready to greet guests, name tags with table assignments are clothespinned to a arbor.

Cindie adorns chandeliers with fresh flowers combining light and loveliness.

An array of hearty breads are paired with bowls of cream cheese flavored with herbs or sundried tomatoes.

A Rustic Wedding

An elegant wedding juxtaposed against a country-classic red barn was both fancy and fun. A warm summer evening added to the setting's perfection, and also inspired the outdoorsy menu. A collection of charcoal cookers produced goat cheese crostini on toasted garlic bread rounds, chicken shish kebabs and other hot-off-the-grill nibbles, When guests sat down for dinner, they feasted on lightly-smoked salmon steaks or beef tenderloin filet.

Another country touch — the bride's mother made jars of homemade jam as take-home gifts for the guests. Each had a party name tag attached.

Blue Cheese Dressing

1/2 large yellow onion, finely chopped

2 cloves garlic, finely chopped

1 cup sour cream

1 cup mayonnaise (Hellman's preferred)

1-1/2 cups good quality French Roquefort cheese, crumbled

Juice of 1 lemon

1 teaspoon salt

1 teaspoon black pepper

2 tablespoons white balsamic vinegar

Combine all ingredients and mix gently. Taste for seasonings and adjust if necessary. Chill until ready to use.

Makes about 4 cups.

TIP | Carve the center out of a small head of lettuce, fill with herbal greens and carrot shreds and serve with blue cheese dressing.

Lightly smoked salmon steaks served with dill dressing, new potatoes and grilled vegetables. See recipe on page 12.

Cucumber-Dill Dressing

2 cucumbers, peeled, seeded and cut into 1/4-inch dice

2 cups mayonnaise

2 cups sour cream

1 small onion, finely diced

1 large garlic clove, finely chopped

1/4 cup finely chopped fresh dill

1 teaspoon freshly ground pepper

1/2 cup white balsamic vinegar

Combine all ingredients in a large bowl. Cover with plastic wrap and place in refrigerator until chilled.

Makes about 6 cups.

DOWN BY THE RIVERSIDE

A couple who enjoyed nature and loved canoeing decided to host their wedding guests at a family cabin next to a pristine Minnesota river. Old boats on the property were transformed into bars and buffets. When guests arrived, they visited the bar boat for Champagne and wine, and then wandered over to a pair of appetizer boats loaded with fish-based snacks such as herring, smoked trout spreads, pickled oysters and salmon pates. Furthering the fishing theme were nets, cattails, crayfish and fishermen's creels. Oil lamps provided illumination as night advanced.

Soile and her crew grilled chicken and beef shish kebabs bright with fresh vegetables. Herbal wild rice was cooked in woks — which then became the serving bowls.

Pickled Oysters

15 small garlic cloves

1 cup thinly sliced carrots

1 cup olive oil

1/2 cup thinly sliced red onion

2 bay leaves

1/2 teaspoon fresh thyme

1/2 teaspoon whole peppercorns

1-1/2 pounds pasteurized shucked small oysters with their juice

1/2 cup thinly sliced sour pickles

1 cup cider vinegar

1/2 cup pickled cocktail onions

1 jalapeno pepper, seeded, sliced into rings

1 lime, sliced

Place garlic and carrots into boiling salted water. Simmer until partially cooked but still crunchy. Heat oil in saucepan; sauté onion for about 5 minutes. Add bay leaves, thyme and peppercorns. Add the oysters and their juice; simmer until edges of oysters curl, about 4 minutes. Remove from heat; cool. Add the pickles, vinegar, onions and jalapeno. Stir in cooked carrots and garlic. Place in glass jar, decorating sides and top of mixture with lime slices. Marinate in the refrigerator for at least 24 hours before serving.

Makes 24 to 30 servings.

What's an outdoor party in Minnesota without mosquitoes?

To ward them off, one table featured a statue of giant biter beside packets of mosquito dope for guests to rub on exposed skin. Problem solved.

Wedding in the Wild

Consider it a trend:

Couples who want to escape the formality of a hotel or church reception are, in ever-greater numbers, looking for a casual rural venue.

This country-style wedding was celebrated on a farm, using an old barn as the setting for the buffet and dancing. As they arrived, guests ducked through a wooden archway decorated with roses and ribbons matching the bridesmaids' dresses.

Emphasis was on garden-fresh, and some of the salad vegetables served were actually picked from the farm's gardens. A visual and flavorful showstopper was a yellow bean and red pepper salad marinated with olive oil, vinegar and fresh herbs. Another favorite was a quinoa-vegetable salad. Soile's signature — a massive fresh fruit display — added elegance. Salmon and beef tenderloins were grilled on site, garnished with herb butter just before serving aside marinated portobello mushrooms, another thrill from the grill.

"It was all very country," said Soile.

Grilled portobello mushrooms marinated with balsamic vinegar, olive oil and garlic.

Yellow beans and red peppers seasoned with white balsamic vinegar and olive oil.

Quinoa salad peppered with fresh vegetables adds a healthy choice.

Quinoa Salad

4 cups ready-made vegetable broth

1-1/2 cups quinoa

1/4 cup white balsamic vinegar

Juice of 2 lemons

1/4 cup olive oil

4 cloves garlic, finely minced

Salt and pepper to taste

1/2 cup sliced Kalamata olives

1/2 cup minced fresh parsley

1/2 cup minced fresh cilantro

1 red onion, finely diced

2 cups halved cherry tomatoes

1 cup diced red pepper

1-1/2 cups crumbled feta cheese

In a large saucepan, combine vegetable broth and quinoa. Cook for 15 to 20 minutes, stirring often, until the quinoa is tender. Drain any excess liquid if necessary, and allow quinoa to cool.

In a small bowl, whisk together the vinegar, lemon juice, olive oil and garlic. Season with salt and pepper.

In a large bowl, combine the cooked and drained quinoa, olives, parsley, cilantro and onion; stir well. Pour on the vinegar dressing mixture. Add the cherry tomatoes, red pepper and feta cheese, tossing until combined. Chill until ready to serve on a platter lined with lettuce leaves.

Makes 24 to 30 servings.

Romanian-born Alexandra Awadeh, who's been a chef alongside Soile for three decades, serves salmon and filet from a buffet where breads nestle in antique wooden bowls.

DOWN ON THE FARM

A bucolic summer wedding set on a suburban farm had a down-home atmosphere applicable to any kind of gathering, especially when budget is limited.

Decor was rustic, with a comfortable, welcoming vibe. Soile rummaged in the barn to find a venerable wooden table which was heaped with greenery and potted plants to greet guests.

Spinach salad with hot bacon dressing (above) and pork tenderloin with sautéed apples and cabbage decorated with roasted red peppers and balsamic vinegar glaze(right).

Then they entered a voluminous barn, where linen-covered tables were topped with economical freshly-sawn boards straight from the lumber yard. Atop the wood was an array of whole grain country loaves plus butter, olive oil and homemade herb cheese for spreading.

Dinner was a sit-down affair, starting with choice of spinach salads (either with hot bacon topping or with strawberries splashed with poppyseed dressing). Two options for the main course: pork tenderloin served with onion, apples and cabbage melange accompanied by Cranberry Pear Chutney (recipe on page 55), or lightly-smoked grilled stuffed rainbow trout (see page 12 for grilling instructions) with new potatoes enriched by Cucumber-Dill Dressing (recipe on page 85). Farmers' markets were an inexpensive source for vegetables, buttered and seasoned.

After the main course was cleared, the wooden slabs were reused, piled with apple and mixed berry crisps, plus bowls of ice cream and billowing whipped cream.

Wooden boxes "planted" with bright flowers were rustic centerpieces.

Coconut Crunchies

2 sticks butter

1 cup sugar

1 cup packed brown sugar

1 teaspoon pure vanilla

2 eggs

2 cups flour

1/2 teaspoon soda

1 teaspoon baking powder

1/4 teaspoon salt

2 cups rolled oats

2 cups cornflakes, lightly crushed

1 cup coconut

Cream butter, sugars and vanilla. Add eggs; mix until well blended. In a bowl, blend flour, soda, baking powder and salt. Add flour mixture to butter mixture. Blend in oats, cornflakes and coconut. Drop dough by teaspoonfuls onto greased baking sheets. Bake at 325 degrees for 15 to 20 minutes, or until golden brown.

Makes about 3 dozen.

Berry crumble and apple crisp were perfect autumnal desserts for a farm wedding.

TIP | Freshly cut tree branches drilled with holes accommodate votive candles.

The bride loved cookies, and as a treat for her guests, jars of homemade favorites were available to sustain energy while dancing to the live band, or for take-home, along with milk in paper cups inscribed with the newlyweds' names and wedding date.

Berry Crumble

2 cups fresh blackberries

2 cups fresh raspberries

2-1/2 cups fresh strawberries, quartered

1/2 cup brown sugar

1/2 cup cornstarch

Zest of 2 lemons

4 tablespoons freshly-squeezed lemon juice

Crumble topping:

3/4 cup almond flour (available at Costco or bakery supply company)

1/2 cup granulated sugar

3/4 cup brown sugar

1/2 cup old-fashioned oats

1 teaspoon ground cinnamon

1 teaspoon ground ginger

1 stick butter, diced

In a large bowl, combine the berries, 1/2 cup brown sugar, cornstarch, lemon zest and lemon juice. In another bowl, stir together the topping ingredients until well mixed and formed into a crumble. In a buttered 9-by-13-inch baking pan, spread the berry mixture. Top with the crumble mixture. Bake at 350 degrees for 40 minutes, until bubbling and the topping is browned. Serve portions warm with whipped cream or ice cream.

Makes 8 to 10 servings.

Gilt-edged Wedding

DINNER MENU

Passed Appetizers Including:

Melon Balls with Prosciutto

Bacon-Wrapped Duck Breast with
Jalapeno Goat Cheese

Seared Sushi Tuna on Wonton Skins

First Course Salad:

Herbal Greens, Poached Pears,
Roquefort, Walnuts, Dried Cranberries
and Raspberry Vinaigrette

Buffet Featuring:

Baked Brie with Blueberries

Abundant Fresh Fruit Arrangement

Assorted Seasonal Salads

Main Course:

Stuffed Chicken Breast

Beef Tenderloin

Roasted Vegetables

Wild Rice Casserole

Wedding Cake:

Celebration Sheet Cake with Fresh Berries

Laura Palmer, whose family owned Stillwater's Lowell Inn for three generations, remains in the hospitality business as coordinator of an events center in Vadnais Heights, north of St. Paul. For her own daughter's wedding, she transformed the center's cavernous spaces into a glittering wonderland. Long swathes of sheer fabric were draped from the ceiling to fill overhead spaces. Rented chandeliers were also draped and decorated with flowers. Golden sashes were tied around covered chairs, and each placesetting was underscored with a gilded charger.

Celebration
Sheet Cake

*Soile's mom's
favorite cake recipe*

3 bakery sheet cake pans

24 eggs

4 cups sugar

3 cups all-purpose flour

3 cups potato flour or cornstarch

3 tablespoons baking powder

Beat eggs and sugar until well-creamed. Slowly add all-purpose flour, potato flour or cornstarch plus baking powder, mixing well after each addition. Line pans with parchment paper and spray well. Divide batter among the pans. Bake in a 350-degree oven for 15 to 20 minutes.

To decorate the cake, whip until stiff 2 quarts heavy cream, sweetening with 2 cups powdered sugar. Place one cake layer on large serving platter. Spread with raspberry jam, then a thick layer of fresh raspberries, pressing them into the jam. Cover with whipped cream. Repeat with another cake layer, jam, berries and cream. Place remaining layer on top and frost all surfaces with whipped cream. Decorate with fresh berries as shown in the photo.

This recipe can be baked in round pans to make a tiered wedding cake as shown in photo on pages 81 and 94.

Makes 100 servings.

TIP | Peel pears; remove core with vegetable peeler and gently poach in water flavored with sugar and fresh lemon juice to keep pears from darkening.

"I love to team with Laura," said Soile. "She has such great vision. And since it was her daughter's wedding, she wanted to make it memorable."

Visually, a triumph!

White Wedding — Wow!

The bride wore white. So did the wedding venue — an historic brownstone building in downtown Minneapolis — where creamy floral displays enhanced the pristine color theme. "The bride had excellent taste, and she and her party coordinator had the vision for the white floral theme, which was so elegant," Soile recalls.

Two hundred guests attending the romantic reception were invited to sample from an array of appetizers as soon as they arrived. They eagerly filled plates with sushi tuna on wonton skins, bacon-wrapped duck breast filled with jalapeno goat cheese, and melon balls wrapped with prosciutto.

When dinner began, the first plate featured tomato basil soup served with heart-shaped grilled cheese sandwiches. Curried Chicken with Couscous was the star of the menu. The wedding cake (recipe on page 93) was filled with chocolate mousse (recipe on page 37). Decorating the whipped cream frosting were harvested-from-the-woods sticks, a simple way to decorate in earthy style, as the couple wished. As guests left, they took with them ribbon-tied bags of heart-shaped ginger cookies covered with a white sugar glaze.

recipe index

Curried Chicken with Couscous

Salad:

3 slices fresh ginger, smashed lightly

3 tablespoons rice wine

2 boneless skinless chicken breasts,
about 1-1/4 pounds

2 tablespoons olive oil

1 teaspoon ground cumin

1 teaspoon salt

1-1/2 cups whole wheat couscous

1 head romaine lettuce, outer leaves removed

4 ribs celery, trimmed, cut into 1/2-inch dice

3 to 4 cups seedless grapes

2 cups fresh pineapple, cut into 1/4 inch dice

1/2 cup minced scallions

1-1/2 tablespoons chopped cilantro

1 cup toasted almonds (optional)

Dressing:

2-inch piece of fresh ginger, peeled and
cut into 1/2-inch pieces

3 cloves garlic, smashed and peeled

2 teaspoons curry powder

2 cups plain yogurt

1 teaspoon salt, or to taste

1/4 teaspoon freshly ground pepper

Juice of 1 lemon

Bring 1 quart water, ginger and rice wine to a boil in a medium saucepan. Add chicken, partially cover, and return to a boil. Reduce heat to medium-low and simmer until chicken is cooked. Remove chicken and let cool, reserving the broth for couscous and dressing.

To prepare couscous: Heat oil in a medium saucepan. Add cumin and sauté over medium-high heat for about 15 seconds. Add 1-1/2 cups reserved chicken broth and salt; cover and bring to a boil. Add couscous. Stir, then remove from heat. Let sit about 5 minutes, then sir with a fork. Cover and set aside.

To prepare dressing: In a food processor, pulse ginger and garlic with steel blade until finely chopped. Add curry powder, yogurt, salt, pepper, lemon juice and 1/2 cup reserved chicken broth. Process until smooth. Adjust seasonings to taste.

To serve salad: Julienne romaine lettuce leaves. Divide among six serving plates. Combine couscous, celery, grapes, pineapple, scallions and cilantro. Add most of dressing, stirring well. Scoop atop lettuce. Slice chicken and arrange over couscous.

Drizzle with remaining dressing. Decorate with pineapple wedges and almonds.

Makes 6 servings.